BIBLE STUDY BASICS

A Closer Look at God's Word

Jeanne Metcalf

Cegullah Publishing & Apologetics Academy
International Copyright © 2024
www.cegullahpublishing.ca
All rights reserved.

ISBN # Textbook: 978-1-998561-02-5
ISBN # Workbook: 978-1-998561-03-2

Cover photo © iStock # 1477629037
Cover design by Jeanne Metcalf.

COPYRIGHT MATTERS

This book is an original manuscript by the author, protected by international copyright laws of Canada. Therefore, no part of this author's work may be reproduced, in part or in whole, or stored in a retrieval system, or transmitted in any form or by any means, electronic, mechanical, photocopied, recorded or otherwise for commercial use without the prior written permission of the author. However, it is possible to receive permission to use short quotations for personal use, or use in a group study, or for permission to copy certain passages, or to make portions of the writings available for overhead viewing. Simply, contact the author to request it.

SCRIPTURE MATTERS

All scripture quotes originate from KJV, public domain. However, the name of God appears as YeHoVaH (or YHVH) not LORD. See Appendix for more information. [1]

---

[1] In this book, we often refer to the day of the LORD. Because this is a well-known term, we did not change LORD to YHVH.

DEDICATION

Dear Reader:

Let me take this moment and commend you for your decision to follow the Lord's command, as written in this scripture:

"Study to show yourself approved unto God, a workman that need not to be ashamed, rightly dividing the word of truth."
                                                                        2 Timothy 2:15

In thanks for your obedience to the scriptures, I, therefore, dedicate this book to "you", dear reader. I know you can only be blessed as you move forward to embrace the principles to correctly divide the Word of truth.

INDEX

CHAPTER	TITLE	PAGE

COURSE 103
Bible Study Basics
Section 1: DISCOVERING ITS AUTHOR

	Introduction	9
1.	Meet the Author	21

Section 2: DISCOVERING ITS ESSENCE

2.	Theme # 1: God Is	35
3.	Theme # 2: Redemption- Part 1	47
4.	Theme # 2: Redemption- Part 2	65
5.	Theme # 2: Redemption- Part 3	77
6.	Themes Conclusion	91

COURSE 104
Bible Study Basics Continued
Section 3: DISCOVERING ITS CONTENTS

7.	Learning Its Structure	99
8.	Grasping Its Precepts	115

Section 4: DISCOVERING ITS TRUTHS

9.	Bible Study Wisdom	129
10.	Bible Study Techniques	139

Section 5: DISCOVERING CHAPTER ANALYSIS

11.	Chapter Analysis Basics	151
	Conclusion	165

CHART INDEX

1. Major Themes of the Bible 61
2. Theme 2 Expanded........................ 62
3. Timeline of the Great & Terrible Day of the LORD…………………………………….. 63
4. Timeline of Day 7……………………… 76
5. CP & AA Inductive Study……………... 163

APPENDIX INDEX

A Name to Honour………………………….. 171
About Jeanne Metcalf………………………. 192
About the King James Version…………….. 177
Books by Jeanne Metcalf…………………… 190
Cegullah Publishing & Apologetics Academy (CP & AA)………………………… 194
CP & AA Faith Statement…………………… 186
Contact Information…………………...……. 195
Salvation's Message………………………….. 178
Scripture Index……………………………….. 183
Sinner's Prayer and Lifetime Commitment… 181

WORD STUDY

Visitation (# 6486)…	58	New (# 2320) …….	108
Visitation (# 1984)…	59	Study (#3854)…….	131
Torah (# 8451)……...	105	Seek (# 1875)……..	133
New (# 2319)……….	108		

COURSE 103
Bible Study Basics

SECTION 1

Discovering Its Author

INTRODUCTION

"The words of the wise are as goads, and as nails fastened by the masters of assemblies, which are given from one shepherd. And further, by these, my son, be admonished: of making many books there is no end; and much study is a weariness of the flesh. Let us hear the conclusion of the whole matter: Fear God, and keep his commandments: for this is the whole duty of man."

Ecclesiastes 12:11-13

AS THE WRITER OF ECCLESIASTES, King Solomon, wrote in his day, *"of making many books there is no end"*. As in Solomon's time, so in ours, for in 2023[2], an estimated 2.2 billion books were published worldwide. Topics of these books, categorized in over 50 genres, included fantasy, science fiction, action and adventure, detective and mystery, thriller and suspense, romance, historical fiction, memoir and autobiography to name a few. Indeed, regarding the study of these books, as King Solomon said, wearies the flesh.

---

[2] UNESCO, June 2023, google search.com.

Bible Study Basics
A Closer Look at God's Word

Revisiting the 2.2 billion books sold in 2023, which includes the Christian genres, we note that Bible sales were at 20 million. That is a good number, and in fact, according to the Book of Guinness World Record 2024, the Bible was the best-selling book of 2023, as well as every year prior[3]. This makes the Bible and its impact on the reading world, impressive.

God's holy book, the Bible, stands out as a unique book in many ways, however, it is excluded from the latter part of Solomon's verse, when he mentioned that the study of many books produces weariness of the flesh. Instead, to study God's Word actually produces life and health to the flesh.

> *Proverbs 4:20-22*
> *"**20** My son, attend to my words; incline thine ear unto my sayings. **21** Let them not depart from thine eyes; keep them in the midst of thine heart. **22** For they are life unto those that find them, and health to all their flesh."*

Truly, to study the Bible fits better in the final part of our verse in Ecclesiastes, *"Fear God, and keep his commandments: for this is the whole duty of man."*

---

[3] Guinness World Records, Jan 4, 2024. Google.com.

Introduction

CHARACTERISTICS OF GOD'S WORD

To delve deeply in the Word of God, is to discover a book like none other.

> *Hebrews 4:12*
> *"For the word of God is quick (living), and powerful, and sharper than any two-edged sword, piercing even to the dividing asunder of soul and spirit, and of the joints and marrow, and is a discerner of the thoughts and intents of the heart."*

Let's take a closer look at what these verses tell us about the Word of God.

A. **God's Word is alive.**

This means that it is not dormant, nor ineffective. It has life within itself and when it is heard, it brings life to its listeners. Yeshua put it this way:

> *John 6:63*
> *"It is the spirit that quickeneth[4]; the flesh profiteth nothing: the words that I speak unto you, they are spirit, and they are life."*

Yeshua's words, which are the words of God, are spirit and life. This means they are eternal!

---

[4] Makes alive.

B. **God's words are powerful, sharper than any two-edged sword.**

A two-edged sword, when used, means business. Thus, this comparison shows us that when God speaks, His Word has a mission to complete. That mission, Isaiah the prophet addressed:

Isaiah 55:11
"So shall my word be that goeth forth out of my mouth: it shall not return unto me void, but it shall accomplish that which I please, and it shall prosper in the thing whereto I sent it."

Since the Word of God is alive, it advances forward from its source with an assignment, which accomplishes its objective.

C. **God's Word hits its target.**

It pierces or breaks through all resistance. It cuts deep, dividing even joints and marrow, soul and spirit. It even separates the thoughts and intents of the heart.

To look at this in greater detail, consider the subject of joint and marrow. Joints are found within the framework of the human skeleton, and the marrow deeply embedded in the joint. Likewise, the soul and the spirit entwine in a

Introduction

strong unity, or a oneness that is as tight as joint and marrow.

That unity of soul and spirit can work together as a positive, *if the two unite in a godly thought*. On the other hand, it can work towards the detriment of the individual, *if the soul and spirit unite in ungodly thoughts and behaviours*[5].

Take for example, a person who find themselves confused about their marriage or frustrated with gender issues, or family matters, or their purpose in life. Reading and listening to God's Word invites the Holy Spirit to come and begin a separation of thoughts and intents of the heart, that which lies within that person's inner most being.

God's Word, acting like a sword, enters their being, moving past all resistance. Its purpose is to help with the sorting process of thoughts, giving opportunity to separate the thoughts to sort through them. In other words, God's Word is so powerful, it pierces the tight unity of the

---

[5] Thoughts and behaviours link together. *Mark 7:21-23 "**21** For from within, out of the heart of men, proceed evil thoughts, adulteries, fornications, murders, **22** Thefts, covetousness, wickedness, deceit, lasciviousness, an evil eye, blasphemy, pride, foolishness: **23** All these evil things come from within, and defile the man."*

soul and spirit. In doing so, it brings to the front the thoughts and intents of the heart. As the Spirit's light enters that person's being their thoughts and feelings becomes exposed to them. Exposing the thoughts and intents of the heart, the Holy Spirit gives opportunity for a change to take place.

Since the Word of God is eternal, living, active and powerful, the essence of the Word keeps on working to help produce a change in the heart of the individual. In this manner, the result of God's Word brings the truth to the surface, whether the person reads a passage relating to their problem or not, the Spirit still speaks, giving guidance.

If that person yields to the leading of the Spirit, their confusion shatters as the Word of God breaks the unity between soul and spirit. If there is no agreement, the Holy Spirit fulfilled an assignment anyway, which was to help the person in areas of right and wrong,[6] etc.

---

[6] *John 16:8 "And when he is come, he will reprove the world of sin, and of righteousness, and of judgment:"*

Introduction

These amazing aspects of God's Word brings us to the conclusion that the Word of God is unique, with an inherent power. There is no other word like it! It is well worth exploring!

EXPLORING GOD'S WORD

To explore God's Word is to embark upon a lifelong journey in pursuit of the greatest treasure on the earth. Walking the road of that journey, then, becomes a paramount experience, since accompanying us on that journey is the Living God, Himself! He graciously walks beside us and willingly extends an invitation to know Him in a deeper, more intimate manner.

Therefore, the journey becomes a time to **connect with the author of the Word!** This is the primary goal! This is the most rewarding goal. Yet, there are other goals worth noting, goals which we will define throughout the chapters of this book. For now, here are a few things to keep in mind.

1. **BEGIN BY READING THE WORD**
    Reading about a subject brings mental enlightenment. As one reads the Word of God, one should:
    - Consider the Holy Spirit as their instructor, their teacher, Who willingly brings His student into His classroom for one-on-one learning.

Bible Study Basics
A Closer Look at God's Word

- Recognize His ability to open the students eyes to truth.
- Trust Him to deposit within the student a love for the truth.

2. CONTINUE TO STUDY THE WORD

Having read the Word, continually, one becomes more proficient, and with proficiency comes a realm of amazing discoveries. Surely, this happens when one:

- Allows the Word to do its job, which is to separate[7] the thoughts and intents of the heart. As that happens, it changes the person for its goal is to make the reader into the image of Yeshua, reflecting His heart, His values, His character, and His love.
- Remembers, the primary role of any student of the Word is to hear and obey[8]! This takes knowing the Word of God seriously, to allow it room to alter the character of its reader.
- Keeps the content of the Word gleaned within its context. *(There are certain safeguards to ensure keeping the integrity of the*

---

[7] Hebrews 4:12

[8] The Word of God regarding hearing the Word, in Hebrew is Strong's # 08085 שמע shama' shaw-mah'. It means to hear and obey.

Introduction

Word. These we will speak about in later chapters.)

- Learns the major principles in the Word of God. As one searches through the Word, we find that there are certain principles of the scripture which never alter. Learning those principles as a foundation, helps to keep integrity in the interpretation of the facts.
- Reaches for the whole counsel of God. Learn to connect each concept with the major ideas of the Word of God, carefully aligning it with where it fits in the bigger picture.

These few things mentioned, here, give the student a heads up on what awaits them as they move ahead to know the Word of God for themselves.

ABOUT BIBLE STUDY BASICS

As you turn the pages of this book, you have an opportunity to learn some basic rules for good Bible study, using an inductive study method. This method, one might explain this way:

Two teachers want to educate their students about the forest in their area.

- Teacher 1 brings into the classroom pictures of animals native to that forest and allows the

students to examine them. Additionally, since it is in the autumn months, she brings to class some different types of leaves. She then teaches the students how to record and tabulate their results.
- Teacher 2, a rather adventurous person, decides to take her students to the forest. There, they can experience the forest for themselves, see the animals firsthand, and collect the fallen leaves, too. Later, after exploring, they hit the books and tabulate their results.

Teacher 2 used the inductive method of learning[9].

TWO GOALS OF INDUCTIVE BIBLE STUDY
Keeping the joy of discovery alive, two major goals make up inductive Bible Study:
- **Goal One**: to encourage a close relationship with the Holy Spirit throughout the learning process. This includes developing an ear to hear the Spirit of the Lord, as the more one reads the Word and spends time with God, the more one learns to hear His Voice. Along side this, one develops a close relationship with God,

---

[9] This book includes a teaching on the inductive study method in Chapter 11. Also, with the purpose of keeping the joy of discovering in the learning process, throughout this book, directly and indirectly, we made reference to inductive study techniques.

Introduction

hopefully seeing Him as best friend, counsellor and confident.
- **Goal Two:** to learn specific guidelines or certain rules of usage to guard against error. This helps to keep inductive study exploration on safe ground. These guidelines we explain throughout the chapters of this book.

We trust that you, dear reader, will glean study tips from this book and develop good study habits. We trust, also, that in the years ahead, as you study the Word of God inductively, you will grow in your understanding of the Word and be blessed by the relationship that awaits you by connecting with that Author of the Word, God, Himself.

Dear reader, it is our prayer for you that you are richly blessed by
Bible Study Basics,
A Closer Look at God's Word.

CHAPTER 1

MEET THE AUTHOR

"6 I am YHVH thy God, which brought thee out of the land of Egypt, from the house of bondage. 7 Thou shalt have none other gods before me."

Deuteronomy 5:6-7

A **MEET THE AUTHOR** event can be an exciting time for both author and audience. Fan numbers escalate as people arrive early, expecting to have their favourite author sign of copy of their work. *But* offer an opportunity to talk to the author, and most fans think that is absolutely over the top!

God, the author of the Word, obviously, will not show up physically at a book signing, but He offers a far better deal! His Omnipresence makes every copy of His Word, *and even fragmented copies*, a wonderful thing to impact generations. Truly, there is none like the

Bible Study Basics
A Closer Look at God's Word

Author of the Bible, Who reaches out to meet every person and takes time, as well, to listen to their every word.

TO KNOW THE GOD OF THE BIBLE
As the Creator of the Universe, God plans to bring every individual near to Him so that they can get to know Him. He wants to embrace each person, connecting with them to help them live the good life upon this earth, which includes an eternal plan with His favour upon them. As such, He reaches out to every individual giving them equal opportunity to know Him.

When one draws near, however, there is a protocol to follow, which the scriptures clearly explain. Simply put[10], human beings must recognize that we all disappoint God, or in Bible words, sin and fall short of God's glory. Therefore, we need a Saviour.

Romans 3:23-26
*"**23** For all have sinned, and come short of the glory of God; **24** Being justified freely by his grace through the redemption that is in Christ Jesus: **25** Whom God hath set forth to be a propitiation through faith in his blood, to declare his righteousness for the remission of sins*

---

[10] If you are not familiar with this protocol, please read the Appendix, Salvation's Message.

Chapter 1
Meet the Author

that are past, through the forbearance of God; **26** *To declare, I say, at this time his righteousness: that he might be just, and the justifier of him which believeth in Jesus."*

God gave us that Saviour: Yeshua. Once we accept Him, and we receive the redemption work He completed on our behalf, we are saved. Through faith, we enter a blood covenant with God, and fully belong to Him. Additionally, we receive His payment of our sins and are given His righteousness. Scripture, then, declares us as just, fully permitted to draw near to God. Yet, that invitation to draw near, differs greatly from the first covenant, when God invited them to come near to Him at Mount Sinai.

A PICTURE OF DRAWING NEAR

Hebrews 12:22-24
*"***22** *But ye are come unto mount Sion, and unto the city of the living God, the heavenly Jerusalem, and to an innumerable company of angels,* **23** *To the general assembly and church of the firstborn, which are written in heaven, and to God the Judge of all, and to the spirits of just men made perfect,* **24** *And to Jesus the mediator of the new covenant, and to the blood of sprinkling, that speaketh better things than that of Abel."*

At Mount Sinai, even though the people were ceremonially sprinkled clean by the blood of a sacrificial animal, they could not come near to God. To do so, meant death. Instead, under the new covenant we can draw near to God without fear because the blood of Yeshua speaks, and it speaks better things than that of the blood of Abel, whose blood cried out for justice.

Here, there is a powerful prophetic picture. In order to understand that prophetic picture, there's a few facts we must investigate.

1. **The Ark of the Covenant.** Under the first covenant, God gave a symbol of His presence. That symbol was called the Ark of His Presence or the Ark of the Covenant.
2. **The Torah.** Inside the Ark of the Covenant, God had Moses place the Torah. This word Torah, best translated as God's instructions for living, contained God's required behaviour for all humankind. Most people know that book today, as the first five books of Moses or the Pentateuch.
3. **The Mercy Seat.** On top of the Ark of the Covenant, sat a special lid called, the Mercy seat. This is where the sacrificial animal blood was sprinkled.

Chapter 1
Meet the Author

Deuteronomy 31:25-26
> **25** *That Moses commanded the Levites, which bare the ark of the covenant of YHVH, saying,* **26** *Take this book of the law, and put it in the side of the ark of the covenant of YHVH your God, that it may be there for a witness against thee.*"

This Torah became a witness to the truth, informing humankind of all that God required of each person. Even so, it could only teach the way of righteousness but could never make a person righteous once they sinned.

Galatians 3:24
> "*Wherefore the Torah was our schoolmaster to bring us unto Christ, that we might be justified by faith.*"

THE PROPHETIC PICTURE
- The Torah outlined God's covenant or commitment to Israel.
- The Torah outlined the terms of the behaviour God expected from Israel within that same covenant agreement. All Israel at Mt. Sinai, agreed to those terms, and thus, the Torah became a witness as to what their agreement with God.

Exodus 24: 6-8
> *"**6** And Moses took half of the blood, and put it in basons; and half of the blood he sprinkled on the altar. **7** And he took the book of the covenant, and read in the audience of the people: and they said, All that the LORD hath said will we do, and be obedient. **8** And Moses took the blood, and sprinkled it on the people, and said, Behold the blood of the covenant, which the LORD hath made with you concerning all these words."*

- The sacrificial blood sprinkled on the mercy seat, when done God's way, made atonement for sin.

However, under the First Covenant, once a person sinned, that covenant required the offended to bring a fresh atonement for sin.

Under the New Covenant, the scenario applies except for one major difference:
- Yeshua's blood was sprinkled on the mercy seat. This blood sacrifice of Yeshua made atonement once and for all!

Hebrews 10: 4-10
> *"**4** For it is not possible that the blood of bulls and of goats should take away sins. **5** Wherefore when he*

cometh into the world, he saith, Sacrifice and offering thou wouldest not, but a body hast thou prepared me: **6** *In burnt offerings and sacrifices for sin thou hast had no pleasure."*

*"**7** Then said I, Lo, I come (in the volume of the book it is written of me,) to do thy will, O God.* **8** *Above when he said, Sacrifice and offering and burnt offerings and offering for sin thou wouldest not, neither hadst pleasure therein; which are offered by the law;* **9** *Then said he, Lo, I come to do thy will, O God. He taketh away the first, that he may establish the second.* **10** *By the which will we are sanctified through the offering of the body of Jesus Christ once for all."*

THE ONLY WAY

So, from the day of Yeshua's death and onward, Yeshua's sacrificial blood testifies of salvation. Therefore, one in Messiah becomes a blood-bought child. The blood of the Lamb testifies to that fact.

Hebrews 12:24
*   **24** And to Jesus the mediator of the new covenant, and to the blood of sprinkling, that speaketh better things than that of Abel."*

With this blood speaking "justified" on the Mercy Seat, the person draws near to God, without fear of death.

These then, are a part of the *"spirits of just men made perfect"*[11].

Through the blood of the Lamb, God shows us the only way to the Father. After we come near to God, everything we received, we received because of Yeshua and the precious blood that He shed on our behalf.

All righteousness, sanctification and redemption came through that precious blood. This eliminates all boasting on the part of the believer because Yeshua attained it all.

NEVER FORGET
Regarding a believer's access to the Almighty, which includes "all blessings in heavenly places[12]," it is imperative to remember that it was gained through Yeshua. Therefore, there is no need to boast.

Remembering from where our righteousness comes, helps to keep one in a humble attitude in their heart and mind. Doing that, makes it easier to receive from the Father, especially when one approaches the Father to embrace truth.

---

[11] *Hebrews 12:23*
[12] *"And hath raised [us] up together, and made [us] sit together in heavenly [places] in Christ Jesus:" Ephesians 2:6*

Chapter 1
Meet the Author

Proverbs 16:18
"Pride goeth before destruction, and an haughty spirit before a fall."

Knowing where we come from, and to Whom we owe our righteousness, propagates a good relationship with God. When it comes to knowing the Word, having a direct connect with God, untainted by pride or a haughty spirit, is imperative.

Ephesians 2:8-9
"8 For by grace are ye saved through faith; and that not of yourselves: [it is] the gift of God: 9 Not of works, lest any man should boast."

Knowing our entrance way to the Father through what Yeshua has done for us, we are ready then to make the most of the invitation to know God. With that accessway open, we are ready to move ahead with our relationship with God. We can now ready ourselves to sit at the feet of our Lord and learn from Him.

This, then, is the
PRIMARY PREREQUISITE
to learning the Word of God!

Bible Study Basics
A Closer Look at God's Word

Dear Reader:

With the accessway to the Father secured, you are now ready to engage in a powerful relationship with your Heavenly Father. With a humble heart, you are, also, ready to be taught by God.

Every believer's relationship differs one from another. However, to study the Bible, successfully, watchfully attend to that relationship between you and YHVH. Remember to keep that relationship, always. Tend to it constantly, to ensure you connect with the author of the Word. Afterall, He knows the Word the best!

In closing, here are some helpful scriptures:

Psalm 73:28
> *"But it is good for me to draw near to God: I have put my trust in the Lord GOD, that I may declare all thy works."*

Psalm 66:18
> *"If I regard iniquity in my heart, the Lord will not hear me:"*

Joshua 23:11
> *"Take good heed therefore unto yourselves, that ye love YHVH your God."*

Psalm 105:1

Chapter 1
Meet the Author

"O give thanks unto YHVH; call upon his name: make known his deeds among the people."

Psalm 93:5

"Thy testimonies are very sure: holiness becometh thine house, O LORD, for ever."

Psalm 119:24

"Thy testimonies also are my delight and my counsellors."

Psalm 119:111

"Thy testimonies have I taken as an heritage for ever: for they [are] the rejoicing of my heart."

Psalm 119:168

"I have kept thy precepts and thy testimonies: for all my ways are before thee."

Psalm 119:129

"PE. Thy testimonies are wonderful: therefore doth my soul keep them."

Bible Study Basics

SECTION 2

Discovering Its Essence

CHAPTER 2

THEME # 1: GOD IS

"[Who] laid the foundations of the earth, [that] it should not be removed for ever."

Psalm 104:5

EVERY WELL WRITTEN BOOK has a theme or a plot. In this respect, the Bible is no exception. To understand the Bible and to come away with the author's intentions, *uncovering the main theme* of the book is *an absolute must.* While there are several mini themes within the Bible, there are *two major themes, with* certain branches within those two major themes. When understood, these two major themes help the ardent student to grasp *the overall message of the Bible.* In this chapter, we will name the two themes, discuss the first theme, and link it with the second theme which we discuss throughout this section.

Let us begin by looking at the first major theme. We find it in the Book of Beginnings, Genesis or *Bereshit*. As this book opens, it introduces the main and most important character of the Bible, God, and at the same time presents the first major theme: *God Is*.

THEME # 1: GOD IS

Genesis 1:1 a
"In the beginning God ..."

This verse introduces the reader to God, and in doing so, states, as a matter of fact, that God is. After all, these first four words of the Bible challenges every reader to recognize that God is or exists. Then, for the remainder of the book, the reader must embrace that statement for the book to make sense.

**Therefore, these first four words
bring a dividing line, pulling no punches.**

If the reader does not believe those first four words, then how would they believe such passages as this one in Isaiah:

Isaiah 41:4
"Who hath wrought and done it, calling the generations from the beginning? I YHVH, the first, and with the last; I am he."

Chapter 2
Theme # 1: God Is

Or, this one in the book of Psalms:

> *Psalm 90:2*
> *"Before the mountains were brought forth, or ever thou hadst formed the earth and the world, even from everlasting to everlasting, thou art God."*

Before anything in our world existed, there was God. He formed the earth and the world! He was before all things and will exist long after all things. In other words, He always was and always will be!

Going back to Genesis 1:1, the bible draws another dynamic picture for us: God moving towards His task of creation.

> *Genesis 1:1-3*
> *"1 ¶ In the beginning God created the heaven and the earth. 2 And the earth **was without form, and void; and darkness [was] upon the face of the deep**[13]. And the Spirit of God moved upon the face of the waters. 3 And God said, Let there be light: and there was light."*

In these early verses of the Bible, we see God approaching total darkness. Neither deterred nor overcome by that darkness, He simply approaches it,

---

[13] Bold and italics added by author.

as it is before Him, *"without form and void"*. These words, "without form and void" tell us that a massive barrenness stood before God, permeated through and through with darkness. Since no light whatsoever existed, literally, God stood before "nothing" but a vast and darkened emptiness.

With His Word, He speaks: "light".

Genesis 1:3
  3 And God said, Let there be light: and there was light."

That one word, which radiated from Him, emerged from His Presence. God's spoken Word and the power within it, right from Day 1, established *His governmental order in the universe, ending darkness and chaos.* Yes, at that very moment, His Word established His government in the earth, and also brought with it, His governmental authority.

Instantly, light divided the darkness. This utter darkness, destitute of all things, quickly moved aside as the Spirit of the living God infused light. God's government, *a government of light* and all associated with it, sprung forth. From then on, God's order ruled the universe![14]

---

[14] This is the beginning of God's Government on the earth.

Chapter 2
Theme # 1: God Is

Next, the Spirit moved upon the face of the deep. This word "moved" constitutes a shaking or vibrating of the mass in front of God. Here, the world begins to take its shape. Skillfully, the Spirit sets in place the various foundational principles of the earth, initialling its energy field, forming, shaping, invigorating all aspects of the earth to meet the needs of its future inhabitants.

With governmental order, through His activities of creation from Day 1 to 6, God created a special place for His greatest creation to exist and flourish. With every special need in mind for His creation, He designed the perfect place for the present and future of the planet we call earth.

> *Isaiah 48:12-13*
> *"**12** Hearken unto me, O Jacob and Israel, my called; I am he; I am the first, I also am the last. **13** Mine hand also hath laid the foundation of the earth, and my right hand hath spanned the heavens: when I call unto them, they stand up together."*

In truth, beginning on Day 1 with the infusion of light. as the Word of God spoke, and then moved upon the face of the deep, intricate aspects of the universe took shape. Then, each day for six days in total, God saw to the establishment of the perfect habitation for His beloved humankind:

- He gave night and day.
- He installed the vault of heaven[15].
- He formed the seas.
- He divided the dry land.
- He brought forth the vegetation.
- He added the sun, moon and stars for signs and seasons and for days and years.
- He brought forth creatures in the seas.
- He gave the earth the winged fowl of the air.
- He brought forth cattle and beasts of the earth.

Up to this point in Genesis, the reader has received two challenges. One, we discussed earlier, God is or exists, and the second one, we see as Genesis 1 continues, presenting God as the creator of all things, including God's prize creation, human beings, which He made in His Image.

Genesis 1:26-27
*"**26** And God said, Let us make man in our image, after our likeness: and let them[16] have dominion over the fish of the sea, and over the fowl of the air, and over the cattle, and over all the earth, and over every creeping*

---

[15] He divided the upper waters from the lower waters and in between placed the expanse of heaven. He prepared it for what we know today including the lower portion where birds fly and the deeper portion where stars, the planets and such would exist.
[16] This word them included Adam, Eve, and their offspring.

Chapter 2
Theme # 1: God Is

thing that creepeth upon the earth. **27** *So God created man in his own image, in the image of God created he him; male and female created he them.*

In this passage, as God continued His work, we see that He sets up earth's government, giving it to "man" (Adam and Eve). We see this in this establishment of earth's government by use of the word, dominion. That word speaks of rulership. Then, God named the specific areas of their dominion:
- *the fish of the sea,*
- *the fowl of the air,*
- *the cattle,*
- *all the earth, including*
- *every creeping thing that creeps upon the earth.*

After He defines the jurisdiction of that dominion, He refers again to that fact that He made them male and female and in the image of God.

Here we see that indeed, God designed a kingdom for His special creation. As God rules and has dominion, so, too, does His creation rule, as He made humankind in His image, capable of ruling.

As Genesis goes on, we see that their rule, which began in complete alignment with God's kingdom, did not remain in that Divine order. Adam and Eve, on a certain day, failed to fulfill their commission to subdue[17] or keep things in God's divine order. Instead, by yielding to the serpent, they opened a door to break that Divine order. In doing so, they came out of agreement with the will of God. Afterwards, through that opened door, sin and death entered the world.

Here begins a second major theme of the Bible:
REDEMPTION.

However, before we look at that theme, let us investigate some important aspects of God's character, which can be seen in the story which recalls the fall[18].

ADAM AND EVE 'S ACCOUTABILITY
Adam and Eve hid from God. God, willing to redeem humankind, exposed the couple's hidden agenda by asking them for their explanation of their behaviour as hid from Him, for at other times, they had fellowship with Him[19].

Genesis 3:12-13
*"**12** And the man said, The woman whom thou gavest to be with me, she gave me of the tree, and I did eat. **13** And YHVH God said unto the woman, What is this*

---

[17] Genesis 1:28
[18] If you are not familiar with that story, please stop here and read Genesis Chapter 3.
[19] Genesis 3:8

that thou hast done? And the woman said, The serpent beguiled me, and I did eat."

Adam, tried to shift blame on God with the words, "the woman you gave me". The woman blamed the serpent. With their comments, we see neither Adam nor Eve desired to take responsibility for their actions. God, however, knowing and understanding the importance of accountability, helped them to see that accountability to God was mandatory.

After helping this couple to recognize their actions were accountable to God, God makes a judgment in the matter, and at the same time, promises humankind redemption.

Genesis 3:15
"And I will put enmity between thee and the woman, and between thy seed and her seed; it shall bruise thy head, and thou shalt bruise his heel."

In this passage, God did not give many specifics regarding this promised "seed", however, here we see that promised seed comes from the woman. History of the Bible shows us "her seed" came! It was the promised Messiah, Yeshua, born of a virgin.

Looking at these things in Genesis 3 and in the verses that follow, we see many interesting things, amongst them:

- **Accountability:**
  - All humankind *(and their governmental order whether it be over their own life or that of others)* give an account to God.
- **Compassion:**
  - Even though they came out of alignment with God's established governmental order and brought sin and death into the world[20], God, nevertheless, had compassion on them. This compassion manifests later, too, as God properly clothed them before they left the Garden.
- **Mercy:**
  - His mercy extends its arms as He removes them from the garden so that they do not eat of the tree of life and thereby remain in a sinful state forever.
- **Supremacy:**
  - His governmental authority triumphs over the divisive plan of the serpent. God had a plan of restoration.

---

[20] *Romans 5:12 "Wherefore, as by one man sin entered into the world, and death by sin; and so death passed upon all men, for that all have sinned:"*

Chapter 2
Theme # 1: God Is

As the story of creation closes, we see God as Redeemer, thus linking this theme with the second one, Redemption. Also, this introduces the reader to a day of great importance which run through the entire Bible, namely, the 7th day

AS REDEEMER:

God's Sovereignty never waned, nor does the fact that He is the Redeemer:

Malachi 3:6
  "For I am YHVH, I change not, therefore, ye sons of Jacob are not consumed."

Isaiah 44:6
  "Thus saith YHVH the King of Israel, and his redeemer YHVH of hosts; I am the first, and I am the last; and beside me there is no God."

THE 7TH DAY:

As the narrative of the 7th day begins, it says:
Genesis 2:2-3
  *"**2** And on the seventh day God ended his work which he had made; and he rested on the seventh day from all his work which he had made. **3** And God blessed the seventh day, and sanctified it: because that in it he had rested from all his work which God created and made."*

Here, we see that God began the 7th day. He ended His work, and He rested from His work. This, by no means says God does not work, for Yeshua tells us that He does:

John 5:17
  "But Jesus answered them, My Father worketh hitherto, and I work."

It means that God rested from His Work of Creation.

Dear Reader, please note that **Genesis 2 never tells us that the seventh day ended,** like it says every other day. Therefore, the Bible makes a clear point here that the 7th day, *the day of the fall of humankind,* continues. That day, however, **is better called,** the day of redemption. That day continues until the time where full redemption of all things transpires and takes place at the time when God makes the heaven and earth anew[21].

---

[21] We will discuss this day further in Chapter 4.

CHAPTER 3

THEME # 2: REDEMPTION PART 1

"Let the words of my mouth, and the meditation of my heart, be acceptable in thy sight, O LORD, my strength, and my redeemer."

Psalm 19:14

THEME # 2: REDEMPTION

FROM GENESIS TO REVELATION, redemption's theme streams, and as it does, it comes because of Theme #1: God Is. Picking up from the close of the last chapter, we recognize God as a redeemer. Earlier, from that chapter, we saw God as a creator, forming humankind. We saw that He set them in a perfect environment, one in which their love, loyalty and obedience to Him would undergo a test. As they underwent this test, God created them sufficient to stand, but free to fall … *and fall they did.*

Yet God, always the perfect Father, never abandoned His creation upon their failure. In fact, He prepared for that day of disobedience.

Revelation 13:8
"And all that dwell upon the earth shall worship him, whose names are not written in the book of life of the Lamb slain from the foundation of the world."

Before the foundation of the world, God's redemptive plan was established, with the Lamb of God slain *before* the foundation of the world[22]. However, for redemption to take place in the lives of God's human creation, as we saw in the last chapter, people must understand their need for accountability.

In that chapter, we saw that when the first couple in the Garden of Eden sinned, they hid from God, but God, in His mercy, called to them. He helped them face the situation. Through that encounter, He taught them how to keep good order in the universe, through acknowledgement of error, or taking responsibility for one's choices. This is important for God required it of them. In other words, God required accountability of them for their actions. Then, He explained His solution to their problem: **REDEMPTION.**

---

[22]Revelation 13:8

Chapter 3
Theme # 2: Redemption- Part 1

ALL CREATION SUFFERED AT THE FALL

The recap of the story of the fall would not be complete, if we did not look at what happened to the remainder of creation.

First, God made skins for His creation:

Genesis 3:21
"Unto Adam also and to his wife did YHVH God make coats of skins, and clothed them."

To clothe them, an animal died. Many scholars believe that, at the time, God showed Adam and Eve how to present a sin offering. After all, later Able, their son, knew well enough to do so. It is more than likely that he learned it from his father, Adam.

Nevertheless, the important fact here is that "death" came into the world when Adam sinned, and that sin effected the animal world. Additionally, according to the Apostle Paul's writing, all creation was affected by Adam's sin.

Romans 8:18-22
*"**18** For I reckon that the sufferings of this present time are not worthy to be compared with the glory which shall be revealed in us. **19** For the earnest expectation of the creature waiteth for the manifestation of the sons*

of God. ***20*** *For the creature was made subject to vanity, not willingly, but by reason of him who hath subjected the same in hope,* ***21*** *Because the creature itself also shall be delivered from the bondage of corruption into the glorious liberty of the children of God.* ***22*** *For we know that the whole creation groaneth and travaileth in pain together until now."*

In simple terms, there is an expectation within creation for a different time coming when God shall deliver them from the bondage of corruption (death). For, according to Paul, all creation groans and travails in pain, together.

Clearly this passage relates that sin in the garden affected all creation, as the death sentence came upon it by default. Thus, all creation agonizes, longing and looking for the time of total redemption from the effects of the fall.

GOD'S REDEMPTIVE SOLUTION UNFOLDS
As Genesis continues and as the First Covenant develops, God's redemptive solution for humankind unfolds in shadows of types. We see this as the author of the New Testament book of Hebrews explains the Tabernacle of Moses, explaining it as a shadow of what was to come.

Chapter 3
Theme # 2: Redemption- Part 1

Hebrews 8:5
"Who serve unto the example and shadow of heavenly things, as Moses was admonished of God when he was about to make the tabernacle: for, See, saith he, that thou make all things according to the pattern shewed to thee in the mount."

Simply put, the things which God gave to Moses were made according to the pattern of the real, (the originals) which Moses saw on the mount. The real are the heavenly ones, and the earthly merely a shadow of the real. God presented it this way to bring an understanding to the surface, *until the real can be understood.*

Among the things God gave Moses, were certain sacrifices, and days of celebration. Colossians refers to those as types and shadows, too.

Colossians 2:16-17
*"**16** Let no man therefore judge you in meat, or in drink, or in respect of an holyday, or of the new moon, or of the sabbath days: **17** Which are a shadow of things to come; but the body is of Christ."*

For sure, when the Second (New) Covenant unfolds, the entire redemptive message escalates to the surface.

That which was hidden in types and shadows moves out of the way as the light of the gospel shines forth.

BASICS OF THE GOSPEL MESSAGE
As an overview of the gospel message[23], it is imperative to recognize **the day of accountability**. This day comes to all, when each person gives an account of what they have done in their life. Also, rulers, or in short, all people who formed governments will give an account to God for what things they did or did not do in their position, for such actions as how they cared for the poor and needy. Did they help them or oppress them? All people, worldwide, in any kind of leadership roles, God expects to govern in the manner that God desires and decrees as righteous.

Take for example, King David. He was an excellent example of a leader in government. He saw himself as an under shepherd appointed by God to care for God's people. His focus in governing, then, centered on ruling in a manner which pleased God. He did not oppress the poor, but rather strove to ensure the poor received fair treatment. He did this because he loved God, loved His Word, and never forgot His precepts.

---

[23] For details about the gospel message, read Salvation's Message in the Appendix.

Chapter 3
Theme # 2: Redemption- Part 1

Psalm 119:140-144
*"**140** Thy word is very pure: therefore thy servant loveth it. **141** I am small and despised: yet do not I forget thy precepts. **142** Thy righteousness is an everlasting righteousness, and thy law is the truth.*
***143** Trouble and anguish have taken hold on me: yet thy commandments are my delights. **144** The righteousness of thy testimonies is everlasting: give me understanding, and I shall live."*

David recognized the One to Whom he must give account for his actions.

On the other hand, King Belshazzar of Babylon had a different viewpoint. In the time of his reign, the hand of God wrote on the wall of his courts, giving him a sentence, condemning him for his behaviour as King. That message came right after he deliberately and intentionally mocked God.

Daniel 5:23-24
*"**23** But hast lifted up thyself against the Lord of heaven; and they have brought the vessels of his house before thee, and thou, and thy lords, thy wives, and thy concubines, have drunk wine in them; and thou hast praised the gods of silver, and gold, of brass, iron, wood, and stone, which see not, nor hear, nor know: and the God in whose hand thy breath is, and whose are all thy*

ways, hast thou not glorified: **24** *Then was the part of the hand sent from him; and this writing was written."*

That message God sent was His judgment. When translated that message declared Belshazzar as having been weighed in God's balance scale and found guilty.

Daniel 5:26-28
*"**26** This is the interpretation of the thing: MENE; God hath numbered thy kingdom, and finished it. **27** TEKEL; Thou art weighed in the balances, and art found wanting. **28** PERES; Thy kingdom is divided, and given to the Medes and Persians."*

This brings us back to accountability to God as seen in the earlier chapter. In that chapter, we saw God teaching Adam and Eve their accountability to Him for their behaviour. In this chapter, we will look at those who rule over others and their accountability to God.

ACCOUNTABILITY TO GOD
Let's begin by looking at God's commandments, the heart of which Yeshua summed up:

Mark 12:30-31
*"**30** And thou shalt love the Lord thy God with all thy heart, and with all thy soul, and with all thy mind, and with all thy strength: this is the first commandment. **31***

Chapter 3
Theme # 2: Redemption- Part 1

And the second is like, namely this, Thou shalt love thy neighbour as thyself. There is none other commandment greater than these."

A good rule of thumb for gaging behaviour comes by examining those behaviours within the measuring stick of these two commandments.
- Love God with all your heart, soul, mind and strength,
- Love your neighbour as you love yourself.

So, when it comes to accountability, no matter the level of authority, be it an individual, a father over a family, an elder over a community, or a ruler over a nation, these laws apply.

THE DAY OF ACCOUNTABILITY
In the book of Hebrews, the author tells us:

Hebrews 9:27
And as it is appointed unto men once to die, but after this the judgment:"

This passage explains the final day of accountability between a person and God. However, the Bible contains other days of accountability, for instance the ones mentioned in the Bible under the term, the day of visitation, or the day of the Lord.

Bible Study Basics
A Closer Look at God's Word

In the book of Isaiah, there is a passage which clearly speaks of the day of visitation, or in modern terms, the day of accountability.

Isaiah 10:1-3
"1 ¶ Woe unto them that decree unrighteous decrees, and that write grievousness which they have prescribed; 2 To turn aside the needy from judgment, and to take away the right from the poor of my people, that widows may be their prey, and that they may rob the fatherless! 3 ***And what will ye do in the day of visitation***[24]*, and in the desolation which shall come from far? to whom will ye flee for help? and where will ye leave your glory?"*

Earlier in Isaiah, God addresses the many ills He has against Israel. Through the prophets He addressed these problems, but they refused to repent and see His face for forgiveness. They refused to turn from their wickedness and return to God and to do what He asked of them. Then as Isaiah 10 opens, God speaks to the leaders, furthering His complaints regarding their behaviour in operating the government and their legal system:
  1. Woe, or sorrow is coming.

---

[24] Bold type by author.

Chapter 3
Theme # 2: Redemption- Part 1

2. It's coming to those who decree, or legislate, unrighteous decrees, or laws.
3. These write grievousness which they have prescribed. In other words, they have written decrees for others which were heinous and dreadful.

Then God names some of the decrees:
4. They turn aside the needy from judgment, and take away the right of my people, meaning they favour the rich and oppress the poor.
5. When it came to judging the causes of widows, they did not care to protect them, nor give them mercy.
6. When the fatherless, (orphans) were judged, they robbed them.

In short, the decrees they made and the judgments they brought forth were corrupt, uncaring, unfair and cruel.

Using the two greatest commands as a measuring stick, God called the governmental leaders into account. As leaders of His people caring for God's sheep, instead of passing righteous decrees, they judged in a manner to financially benefit themselves and others who were wealthy, at the expense of the poor and needy of the land.

To these rulers, God asks a question, "What will you do in the day of visitation?" These rulers may have judged in favour of the rich and for those who could benefit them, but when the time came for giving an account to God, they could not call in those favours! No, in the day of accountability when God requires it of them, no one could champion their cause for they made unrighteousness their companion instead of God's laws and precepts.

We see this accountability in both the Hebrew (found in Isaiah 10: 3 and other passages) and Greek word (as found in 1 Peter 2:12) and translated as visitation:

Isaiah 10:3
   3 And what will ye do in the day of visitation[25], and in the desolation which shall come from far? to whom will ye flee for help? and where will ye leave your glory?"

Word	Strong's Number	Hebrew
Visitation	6486	פְּקֻדָּה Pronounced pëquddah
Meaning: to visit upon or punish. Amongst its meanings is the word, account, as to give an account.		

---

[25] Bold type by author.

Chapter 3
Theme # 2: Redemption- Part 1

1 Peter 2:12

"Having your conversation (behaviour) honest among the Gentiles: that, whereas they speak against you as evildoers, they may by your good works, which they shall behold, glorify God in the day of visitation."

Word	Strong's Number	Greek
Visitation	1984	ἐπισκοπή pronounced episkope
Meaning. that act by which God investigates and searches out the ways, deeds character, of men, to adjudge them their lot accordingly, whether joyous or sad.		

In other words, the day of visitation is the day of accountability. That day comes to every person, and in its season, to every ruler of every nation[26]. As each one stands before His creator, whether they have acknowledged God or not, they will give an account in accordance with God's measuring stick.

This is where the gospel message comes in. Those in Messiah already know the guilt of their sin as well as the death sentence they well deserve, BUT DUE TO GOD'S MERCY, through Yeshua, their debt of sin was paid in full.

---

[26] This includes a one world order!

Therefore, on the day of accountability, whenever it comes, there will be two groups. When it comes to nations, either goat or sheep nations, but their rulers will fall into the same category as individuals:
- Recipients of God's Grace:
    o Recognized, earlier, their accountability to God.
    o Took care of the sin problem, God's way, bringing the acceptable sin offering.
- Rejectors of God's Grace:
    o Refused accountability to God.
    o Rejected God's plan to take care of sin, refusing to bring the acceptable sin offering.

On the day of visitation, whether the Bible identifies it that way, or the Day of the Lord, God brings people into account for their actions.

***

CHARTS ON THE NEXT THREE PAGES:
Chart 1 is a recap of Chapter 2 and Chapter 3.
Chart 2 which expands the timeline of Theme # 2 and Chart 3 is covered in Chapter 4.

Chapter 3
Theme # 2: Redemption- Part 1

CHART # 1: Major Themes of the Bible

THEME:	GOD IS	
	God's Government Established (day 1) Genesis 1:1-3	Earth's Government Established (day 6) Genesis 1:26-28
	CREATOR, SOVEREIGN RULER, FATHER TO ALL HUMANKIND, REDEEMER	
	"For I am the LORD, I change not; therefore, ye sons of Jacob are not consumed." (Malachi 3:6)	

THEME:	REDEMPTION (Day 7)			
	ACCOUNTABILITY TO GOD (Genesis 2:15-17)			
	ALL ARE ACCOUNTABLE TO GOD, INCLUDING GOVERNMENTS			
Individuals	Families	Communities	Individual Nations	All Nations (1 world order)
All will face a Day of Accountability				
In preparation for that Day, God speaks about:				
Recipients of God's Mercy			Recipients of God's Justice/Wrath	
Whosoever will, may come.				
Recipients of God's Grace:			Rejectors of God's Grace:	
Recognize as accountable to God.			Refuse accountability to God.	
Take care of sin God's Way:			Won't take care of sin God's way.	
Accept God's plan to take care of sin.			Reject God's plan to take care of sin.	
Bring required Sin offering.			Do not bring required Sin offering.	
Look for Messiah (1st Covenant)			Have own theories	
Look for return of Messiah (Yeshua) (2nd Covenant)			Reject it all	

COPYRIGHT CP & AA 2024

Bible Study Basics
A Closer Look at God's Word

CHART # 2: Theme 2 Expanded

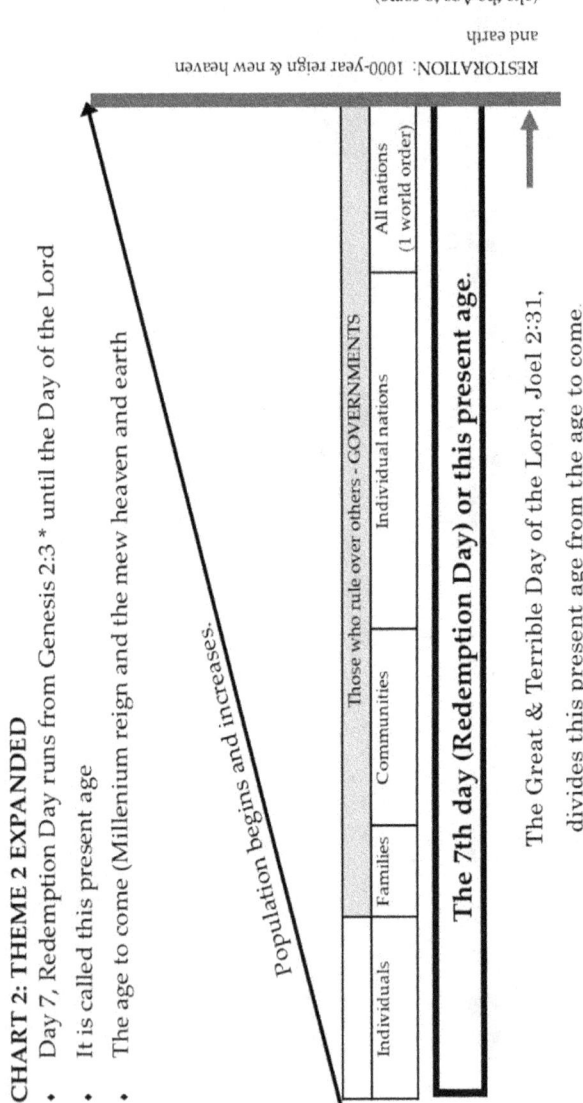

CHART 2: THEME 2 EXPANDED
- Day 7, Redemption Day runs from Genesis 2:3 * until the Day of the Lord
- It is called this present age
- The age to come (Millenium reign and the new heaven and earth

* Note: Genesis 2:3 announces day when God rested from His work of creation, but it never says the day ends like every other day in creation.

COPYRIGHT CP & AA 2024

Chapter 3
Theme # 2: Redemption- Part 1

CHART # 3: Timeline of Great & Terrible Day of the LORD

REMEMBER:

The Great and Terrible Day of the Lord ends this age, (or 7th day).

HOWEVER,

Scripture speaks of times which are prophetic pictures to the Day of the Lord.:

As an individual (at time in life when their cup of iniquity is full, and/or their day of judgment comes.

As a governing body, (families, communities, individual nations, all nations (one world order) – God brings them into account for what has been done, with rewards for good or evil as per the timeframe. (E.G. the Flood, Babel, Assyria, Babylon, etc.)

These days of accountability are prophetic to THE GREAT AND TERRIBLE DAY OF THE LORD.

THE GREAT AND TERRIBLE DAY OF THE LORD	
	It brings with it
Reward of the Righteous	Reward of the wicked

AFTERWARDS COMES THE RESTORATION OF ALL THINGS	
All creation is redeemed (Romans 8:29-22)	1 Corinthians 15:55 (Death swallowed up in victory)
1000-year reign	Creation of new Heaven and Earth
	Revelation 21:1 and onward

COPYRIGHT CP & AA 2024

As addressed, there are two major themes in the Bible, each one branching out with themes within a theme. While we have not explored those themes within Theme # 1, we will explain a few themes with Theme # 2. Theme # 2, Redemption Theme, which we discussed in the last chapter, includes the 7th day of Creation, and the theme of the Day of the Lord. The first in the subject of Chapter 4, and the latter is the subject of Chapter 5.

CHAPTER 4

THEME 2: REDEMPTION
PART 2

IN THIS CHAPTER, we will pick up the 7th Day (Redemption Day) and explain the terms "present age". Then, in Chapter 5, we will discuss the Day of the LORD in more detail, as well as its place in the timeline.

DAY 7, (REDEMPTION DAY)
In the account of creation, when referring to each day and what had transpired, it looks back to the day, making this statement:

"And the evening[27] and the morning were" and then inserts the day.

---

[27] Note: In the Hebrew mindset, the evening came first, after all darkness was here until God said, "Light".

Thus, the Bible makes it clear, each day began and ended.

Genesis 1:5
And God called the light Day, and the darkness he called Night. And the evening and the morning were the first day.

Genesis 1:8
And God called the firmament Heaven. And the evening and the morning were the second day.

Genesis 1:13
And the evening and the morning were the third day.

Genesis 1:19
And the evening and the morning were the fourth day.

Genesis 1:23
And the evening and the morning were the fifth day.

Genesis 1:31
And God saw every thing that he had made, and, behold, it was very good. And the evening and the morning were the sixth day

Chapter 4
Theme # 2: Redemption- Part 2

Moving on to the 7th Day, the Bible says,

Genesis 2:1-3
*"**1** ¶ Thus the heavens and the earth were finished, and all the host of them. **2** And on the seventh day God ended his work which he had made; and he rested on the seventh day from all his work which he had made. **3** And God blessed the seventh day, and sanctified it: because that in it he had rested from all his work which God created and made."*

After this, the seventh day of creation is no longer mentioned, however, we are given a closer account of the creation of humankind, as well as a recap of the fall in Chapter 3. Regarding the 7th day, we recognize that:
1. God rested from His work of creation and thus, it is a day of Rest.
2. It is a blessed day.
3. It is a day which is set apart from all other days.

DAY OF REST
This, by no means says God does not work, for Yeshua tells us that He does[28]:

John 5:17
"But Jesus answered them, My Father worketh hitherto, and I work."

---

[28] Here we pick up the theme from Chapter 1, as promised.

Bible Study Basics
A Closer Look at God's Word

This means that God rested from His Work of Creation. It also means that when God finished His work, He had no intentions of creating another day, at that point. Obviously, He knew mankind would sin and He prepared the Lamb of God for that situation[29]. Now, God rested from His work of creation because He had a plan to redeem the situation, set in place *prior* to the foundation of the world[30].

Humankind can take a lesson from God's rest, in that one must enter the rest of God to receive the plan of redemption for their life. Through the promised Lamb, believers receive righteousness as a free gift:

Romans 5:18
"*Therefore as by the offence of one judgment came upon all men to condemnation; even so by the righteousness of one the free gift came upon all men unto justification of life.*"

We know that works for merit towards salvation does not cut it with God. One rests from their own works and trusts God! Additionally, everything in Messiah one receives by faith, as faith is a place where one rests and trusts God to do as He promised.

---

[29] Revelation 13:8
[30] Revelation 13:8

Chapter 4
Theme # 2: Redemption- Part 2

A BLESSED DAY
Again, God knew the entrance of sin and death was coming, yet He still blessed the day. After the fall, He never cursed the day, either. God cursed the serpent[31]. He cursed the ground for humankind's sake[32].

However, contrary to what some teach, He neither cursed Adam nor Eve. Instead, He blessed them with His redemptive message, a message which continues throughout day 7, until the dawning of the Day of Vengeance, or the Day of the LORD.

IT IS A DAY WHICH IS SET APART (SANCTIFIED)
This day, He set apart from all other days, or He sanctified the day. Something sanctified is something put aside and given to God. In other words, the day belongs to God.

To some this might seem strange because of the latter activities in the day when sin and death entered. However, God blessed the day and would not discard His blessing nor the creation which He made, including the one He called, "very good".

---

[31] *Genesis 3:14*
[32] *Genesis 3:17*

Genesis 1:31
"And God saw every thing that he had made, and, behold, it was very good. And the evening and the morning were the sixth day."

Rather than discard the creation which fell, God reached out to them, promising redemption. Knowing this day would come, knowing the pain, agony and sorrow to come, far better than Adam and Eve could even imagine, God blessed humankind with so great a salvation as we know, today, through salvation. This day, the day of rest, then, became the day of promised redemption!

7TH DAY CONTINUES
Keeping in mind the fact that Genesis 2 never closed day 7, and as the record of that day continued into Chapter 3 where God promised redemption, we see how God looks at the 7th day. He looks at is as the

DAY OF REDEMPTION.

So, as long as day 7 transpires, redemption is possible. This day, then, defines the day in which we live, or to put it another way, the age in which we live. Humankind lives within this age until the age to come arrives. That age Yeshua spoke about:

Chapter 4
Theme # 2: Redemption- Part 2

Matthew 12:32
"And whosoever speaketh a word against the Son of man, it shall be forgiven him: but whosoever speaketh against the Holy Ghost, it shall not be forgiven him, neither in this world, neither in the world to come."

Here the word for "world" can better be interpreted as "age". Therefore, the latter part of the verse should read. *"Neither in this age, neither in the age to come"*.

That is the time of restoration of all things, the time of the new heaven and earth:

Revelation 21:1-5
"1 And I saw a new heaven and a new earth: for the first heaven and the first earth were passed away; and there was no more sea. 2 And I John saw the holy city, new Jerusalem, coming down from God out of heaven, prepared as a bride adorned for her husband. 3 And I heard a great voice out of heaven saying, Behold, the tabernacle of God is with men, and he will dwell with them, and they shall be his people, and God himself shall be with them, and be their God. 4 And God shall wipe away all tears from their eyes; and there shall be no more death, neither sorrow, nor crying, neither shall there be any more pain: for the former things are passed away. 5 And he that sat upon the throne said, Behold, I

make all things new. And he said unto me, Write: for these words are true and faithful."

As we look forward to this age, while living in this present age, day 7, or day of Redemption, we know 2 things:

- Redemption is promised. Therefore, we proclaim the gospel message to invite the "whosoever will" to come.
- Look forward to the age to come when, as verse 3 and 4 describes:
    - *3 And I heard a great voice out of heaven saying, Behold, the tabernacle of God is with men, and he will dwell with them, and they shall be his people, and God himself shall be with them, and be their God.*
    - *4 And God shall wipe away all tears from their eyes; and there shall be no more death, neither sorrow, nor crying, neither shall there be any more pain: for the former things are passed away."*

Until the "age to come" **this present age**, Day 7, redemption day, continues with:
- Death
- Sorrow
- Crying

Chapter 4
Theme # 2: Redemption- Part 2

- Pain
- and such things such as violence, injustice, cheating, stealing, and oppression, etc.

During **this present age,** God upholds the cause of the oppressed:

Psalm 9:11-18
"11 ¶ *Sing praises to YHVH, which dwelleth in Zion: declare among the people his doings. 12 When he maketh inquisition for blood, he remembereth them: he forgetteth not the cry of the humble. 13 Have mercy upon me, O LORD; consider my trouble [which I suffer] of them that hate me, thou that liftest me up from the gates of death: 14 That I may shew forth all thy praise in the gates of the daughter of Zion: I will rejoice in thy salvation.*

15 The heathen are sunk down in the pit [that] they made: in the net which they hid is their own foot taken. 16 The LORD is known [by] the judgment [which] he executeth: the wicked is snared in the work of his own hands. Higgaion. Selah. 17 The wicked shall be turned into hell, [and] all the nations that forget God. 18 For the needy shall not alway be forgotten: the expectation of the poor shall [not] perish for ever."

From this passage we see, regarding the oppressed, that God:
- Remembers the cry of the humble.
- Considers those in trouble, who cry out to Him when they suffer by them who hate them.
- Lifts those suffering from the gates of death, who show forth all His praise and rejoice in His salvation.
- Turns the tables on those unrighteous (here called heathens) so that the net which they hid for the righteous, traps the wicked.

This Psalm goes on to say that YeHoVaH:
- executes judgment on the wicked, snaring them in the work of their own hands.
- Sees that the wicked are turned into hell, as well as all the nations that forget God.

As the Psalm nears its end, it says that the needy shall not always be forgotten and the expectation of the poor shall not perish for ever.

While this Psalm of David petitions God regarding things in the king's life and the issues of his day, it shows us David's expectations from YeHoVaH. David knows God as the deliverer and well able to champion the causes of those in need, a theme about which he spoke earlier in the Psalm.

Chapter 4
Theme # 2: Redemption- Part 2

Psalm 9: 7-10
"7 But YHVH shall endure for ever: he hath prepared his throne for judgment. 8 And he shall judge the world in righteousness, he shall minister judgment to the people in uprightness. 9 The LORD also will be a refuge for the oppressed, a refuge in times of trouble. 10 And they that know thy name will put their trust in thee: for thou, LORD, hast not forsaken them that seek thee."

King David speaks here of God as a Judge who ministers judgment to the people uprightly. He sees God as a place of refuge for the oppressed in times of trouble for those who put their trust in YeHoVaH. God will not forsake those that seek Him.

Clearly, David sees God as a champion of the downtrodden, the oppressed and the needy. He trusts God to righteously judge their cause, knowing that YeHoVaH rules in favour of righteousness. As David knows, God is not swayed by words, and His eyes are not blind to oppressors. God will judge in uprightness.

As we close out this chapter, remember that God understands the dynamics upon the earth. He carefully weighs out circumstances and when God acts, His actions are just. Therefore, in the day of Vengeance, in the Day of the LORD, God shall judge in complete understanding with the proper measures of justice served.

CHART # 4: Timeline of Day 7

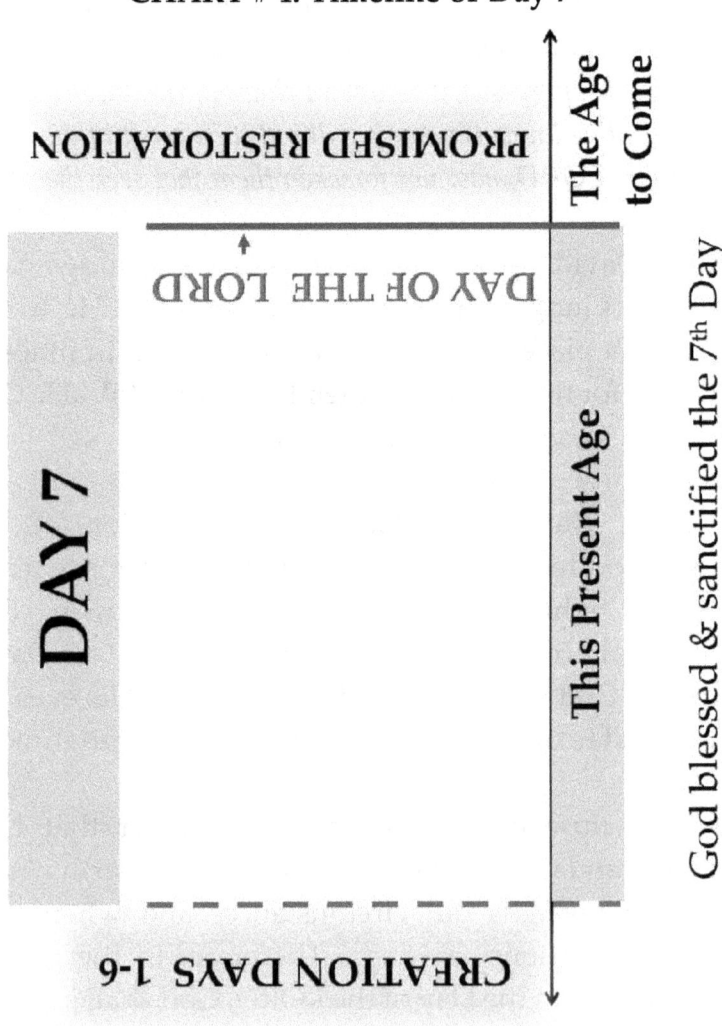

CHAPTER 5

THEME 2: REDEMPTION PART 3

"And I will restore to you the years that the locust hath eaten, the cankerworm, and the caterpiller, and the palmerworm, my great army which I sent among you."

Joel 2:25

ACCORDING TO YESHUA, we have two ages:
- This present age, and
- The age to come.[33]

What is the dividing line between the 2 ages?

It is the Day of the Lord,

as seen in the last chapter, and in the chart, entitled, "Timeline of Day 7" on the previous page.

---

[33] Matthew 12:32

THE DAY OF THE LORD

Isaiah, Jeremiah, Ezekiel, Joel, Amos, Obadiah, Zephaniah, Zechariah, and Malachi, prophets of the first covenant, all spoke of the Day of the Lord. Through these prophetic passages we glean a little about that day.

> *Isaiah 2:12-18*
> *"**12** For the day of the LORD of hosts shall be upon every one that is proud and lofty, and upon every one that is lifted up; and he shall be brought low: **13** And upon all the cedars of Lebanon, that are high and lifted up, and upon all the oaks of Bashan, **14** And upon all the high mountains, and upon all the hills that are lifted up, **15** And upon every high tower, and upon every fenced wall, **16** And upon all the ships of Tarshish, and upon all pleasant pictures[34]. **17** And the loftiness of man shall be bowed down, and the haughtiness of men shall be made low: and YHVH alone shall be exalted in that day. **18** And the idols he shall utterly abolish."*

Here, defined further as the day of the Lord of Hosts, (YHVH Tseva'ot), it shows those affected by the day:
- Everyone that is proud and lofty; upon everyone that is lifted up, they shall be brought low.

---

[34] Watch towers.

Chapter 5
Theme # 2: Redemption- Part 3

- All cedars of Lebanon, that are high and lifted up, and upon all the oaks of Bashan.
- Upon all the high mountains and upon the hills that are lifted up.
- Upon every high tower and upon every fenced wall.
- Upon all the ships of Tarshish and all pleasant watch towers.

Verse 17 gives us the bottom line of this word:
- The loftiness of man shall be bowed down.
- The haughtiness of men shall be made low.
- YHVH alone shall be exalted in that day.
- All idols, He shall utterly abolish.

In short, everything that human beings trust in, other than God, shall be affected. Their worth shall be shown for what it was, too, no refuge in the day of trouble.

Isaiah 13:6-9
"6 ¶ Howl ye; for the day of the LORD is at hand; it shall come as a destruction from the Almighty. 7 Therefore shall all hands be faint, and every man's heart shall melt: 8 And they shall be afraid: pangs and sorrows shall take hold of them; they shall be in pain as a woman that travaileth: they shall be amazed one at another; their faces shall be as flames. 9 Behold, the day

of the LORD cometh, cruel both with wrath and fierce anger, to lay the land desolate: and he shall destroy the sinners thereof out of it."

Here we see come with great sorrow, for Isaiah's audience is told to howl, for it is at hand, and it comes as a destruction from the Almighty.

- All hands shall faint.
- Every person's heart will melt
- They shall be afraid, and so much so that they will resemble a woman with intense labour pains.
- They shall be amazed at one another how they react with such fear.

Then Isaiah says, look, the day of the LORD comes cruel with wrath and fierce anger to lay the land desolate. God will destroy the sinners (unrighteous) out of the land.

Isaiah continues his prophecy saying:

Isaiah 13:10-13
*"**10** For the stars of heaven and the constellations thereof shall not give their light: the sun shall be darkened in his going forth, and the moon shall not cause her light to shine. **11** And I will punish the world*

Chapter 5
Theme # 2: Redemption- Part 3

for their evil, and the wicked for their iniquity; and I will cause the arrogancy of the proud to cease, and will lay low the haughtiness of the terrible. **12** *I will make a man more precious than fine gold; even a man than the golden wedge of Ophir.* **13** *Therefore I will shake the heavens, and the earth shall remove out of her place, in the wrath of YHVH of hosts, and in the day of his fierce anger."*

Here we see:
- The stars of heaven and the constellations shall not give their light.
- The sun shall be darkened.
- The moon won't give its light.
- God shall punish the world for their evil and the wicked for their iniquity.
- He will cause the arrogancy of the proud to cease and lay low the haughtiness of the terrible.
- Humankind will be as rare as fine gold.
- He will shake the heavens.
- The earth shall move out of her place.

All this happens in the wrath of YHVH Tseva'ot in the day of his fierce anger.

As Isaiah continues, he further adds to the day of the LORD, only he calls it the indignation of YHVH.

Isaiah 34:1-4
> *"**1** Come near, ye nations, to hear; and hearken, ye people: let the earth hear, and all that is therein; the world, and all things that come forth of it. **2** For the indignation of YHVH is upon all nations, and his fury upon all their armies: he hath utterly destroyed them, he hath delivered them to the slaughter. **3** Their slain also shall be cast out, and their stink shall come up out of their carcases, and the mountains shall be melted with their blood. **4** And all the host of heaven shall be dissolved, and the heavens shall be rolled together as a scroll: and all their host shall fall down, as the leaf falleth off from the vine, and as a falling fig from the fig tree."*

As the chapter continues, Isaiah continues to describe the horrors of that day.

In summary of these and other passages from Isaiah, note how the narrative begins with a narrowed day of accountability, such as the destruction of the cedars of Lebanon, to a wider scope of all nations, at which time there comes a shaking of the heavens and earth. In other words, in prophesying to the punishment of the nation, Isaiah broadens the scope to include a larger, far-reaching area of God's wrath. As he prophesied, he broadened the day into a day which is wider and all inclusive of the entire world.

Chapter 5
Theme # 2: Redemption- Part 3

Other prophets did the same, one of them being Joel.

> Joel 1: 15-20
> "**15** Alas for the day! for the day of the LORD is at hand, and as a destruction from the Almighty shall it come. **16** Is not the meat cut off before our eyes, yea, joy and gladness from the house of our God? **17** The seed is rotten under their clods, the garners are laid desolate, the barns are broken down; for the corn is withered. **18** How do the beasts groan! the herds of cattle are perplexed, because they have no pasture; yea, the flocks of sheep are made desolate. **19** O LORD, to thee will I cry: for the fire hath devoured the pastures of the wilderness, and the flame hath burned all the trees of the field. **20** The beasts of the field cry also unto thee: for the rivers of waters are dried up, and the fire hath devoured the pastures of the wilderness."

Joel starts out with the day of the Lord is at hand, even a destruction from the Almighty. Then, he shows how it will affect the local scene:
- Meat is cut off before our eyes.
- Joy and gladness from the house of our God.
- The seed is rotten, the storehouses empty, the barns where they stored food broken down.
- The corn is withered.

- The beasts of the earth groan and are perplexed because of the lack of food, and the sheep of the field are desolate.
- Fire devoured the pastures of the wilderness, and the flame burned all the trees of the field.
- The beasts cry out to God for the rivers of waters are dried up.
- Fires have devoured the pastures of the wilderness.

In Joel 2, he continues his narrative, calling the inhabitants of the land to tremble because the day of the Lord is near.

Joel 2:1-9

> *"1 ¶ Blow ye the trumpet in Zion, and sound an alarm in my holy mountain: let all the inhabitants of the land tremble: for the day of the LORD cometh, for it is nigh at hand; 2 A day of darkness and of gloominess, a day of clouds and of thick darkness, as the morning spread upon the mountains: a great people and a strong; there hath not been ever the like, neither shall be any more after it, even to the years of many generations. 3 A fire devoureth before them; and behind them a flame burneth: the land is as the garden of Eden before them, and behind them a desolate wilderness; yea, and nothing shall escape them. 4 The appearance of them is as the appearance of horses; and as horsemen, so shall they run. 5 Like the noise of chariots on the tops of*

Chapter 5
Theme # 2: Redemption- Part 3

> *mountains shall they leap, like the noise of a flame of fire that devoureth the stubble, as a strong people set in battle array. **6** Before their face the people shall be much pained: all faces shall gather blackness. **7** They shall run like mighty men; they shall climb the wall like men of war; and they shall march every one on his ways, and they shall not break their ranks: **8** Neither shall one thrust another; they shall walk every one in his path: and when they fall upon the sword, they shall not be wounded. **9** They shall run to and fro in the city; they shall run upon the wall, they shall climb up upon the houses; they shall enter in at the windows like a thief.*

Joel's described that day as a dark and gloomy scene. He speaks of a great army coming like nothing ever seen before. A fire burns up the area and that which once looked like a garden of Eden becomes a desolate wilderness. Nothing escapes that army! Joel continues to describe them as unstoppable.

His narrative continues:

Joel 2:10-11
> *10 The earth shall quake before them; the heavens shall tremble: the sun and the moon shall be dark, and the stars shall withdraw their shining: 11 And YHVH shall utter his voice before his army: for his camp [is] very great: for [he is] strong that executeth his word:*

for the day of the LORD [is] great and very terrible; and who can abide it?"

Joel speaks of the "earth" quaking before them, and the heavens trembling with the sun and moon darkening, and the stars not giving their light. At that point, Isaiah describes YHVH as uttering His voice before His army, for His camp is great, for the day of the Lord is great and very terrible. Who can stand it?

Looking at Joel 2 further on, continuing his prophetic word, he says,

Joel 2:27-31
*"**27** And ye shall know that I am in the midst of Israel, and that I am YHVH your God, and none else: and my people shall never be ashamed. **28** ¶ And it shall come to pass afterward, that I will pour out my spirit upon all flesh; and your sons and your daughters shall prophesy, your old men shall dream dreams, your young men shall see visions: **29** And also upon the servants and upon the handmaids in those days will I pour out my spirit. **30** And I will shew wonders in the heavens and in the earth, blood, and fire, and pillars of smoke. **31** The sun shall be turned into darkness, and the moon into blood, before the great and the terrible day of the LORD come."*

Chapter 5
Theme # 2: Redemption- Part 3

Continuing with his theme, Joel speaks of those who trust in God, promising the good that God brings. Then, He concludes with further comments regarding the day of the LORD, calling that day "great and terrible".

Luke, the author of the book of Acts, quotes Peter, the apostle, as using this passage in his address to a listening audience at Shavuot (Pentecost):

Acts 2:16-21
> *"**16** But this is that which was spoken by the prophet Joel; **17** And it shall come to pass in the last days, saith God, I will pour out of my Spirit upon all flesh: and your sons and your daughters shall prophesy, and your young men shall see visions, and your old men shall dream dreams: **18** And on my servants and on my handmaidens I will pour out in those days of my Spirit; and they shall prophesy: **19** And I will shew wonders in heaven above, and signs in the earth beneath; blood, and fire, and vapour of smoke: **20** The sun shall be turned into darkness, and the moon into blood, before that great and notable day of the Lord come: **21** And it shall come to pass, that whosoever shall call on the name of the Lord shall be saved."*

This message Peter applied to explain what happened on the day of Pentecost. Here he quotes Joel regarding the outpouring of the Holy Spirit, referring to God showing wonders in the heaven and signs in the earth.

Obviously, Peter perceived some of these signs had transpired, perhaps referring to the sky darkening and the earth quaking at Yeshua's crucifixion and death[35]. While it is possible that a solar eclipse took place and later an earthquake, the sun was not completely turned to darkness and the moon into blood, as Joel prophesied regarding the great and terrible day of the Lord.

Peter's application was correct in the way he intended it and applied it, *however, considering the words of Yeshua,* **that prophetic word** *has a greater fulfilment just before His return to the earth to set up His kingdom and bring in the millennium reign.*

---

[35] *Matthew 27:50-53 "***50** *Jesus, when he had cried again with a loud voice, yielded up the ghost.* **51** *And, behold, the veil of the temple was rent in twain from the top to the bottom; and the earth did quake, and the rocks rent;* **52** *And the graves were opened; and many bodies of the saints which slept arose,* **53** *And came out of the graves after his resurrection, and went into the holy city, and appeared unto many."*

Chapter 5
Theme # 2: Redemption- Part 3

Matthew 24:29-31
*"**29** Immediately after the tribulation of those days shall the sun be darkened, and the moon shall not give her light, and the stars shall fall from heaven, and the powers of the heavens shall be shaken: **30** And then shall appear the sign of the Son of man in heaven: and then shall all the tribes of the earth mourn, and they shall see the Son of man coming in the clouds of heaven with power and great glory. **31** And he shall send his angels with a great sound of a trumpet, and they shall gather together his elect from the four winds, from one end of heaven to the other."*

CONCLUSION

As prophets prophesied, while they called to a people and/or a nation for times of judgment, *at the same time*, they presented, through their prophetic word, a broader picture of the *final* day of the LORD, also in places, calling it, "that great and terrible day". That final day, however, divides the 7th day from the day of restoration. That is the day when God comes, and His reward is with Him:

- **Reward of the righteous for their righteousness and**
- **the reward for the unrighteous for their unrighteousness.**

In the meantime, every day of accountability prophesied brings with it an opportunity for people and nations to repent and return to YeHoVaH. Surely, He desires that all know Him:

2 Peter 3:9
"The Lord is not slack concerning his promise, as some men count slackness; but is longsuffering to us-ward, not willing that any should perish, but that all should come to repentance."

Thus, the reason for many earlier manifestations or rehearsals to the Day of the LORD:

God's Mercy desires that all be saved.
He extends His plea to all repent!
It is a "whosoever will may come" opportunity.

CHAPTER 6

THEMES CONCLUSION

"All scripture [is] given by inspiration of God, and [is] profitable for doctrine, for reproof, for correction, for instruction in righteousness:"

2 Timothy 3:16

IN THIS SECTION, entitled Discovering Its (the Bible's) Realities we looked at the two major themes of the Bible that run from Genesis to Revelation:
1. God is.
2. Redemption.

THEME # 1: GOD IS
When discussing Theme # 1, we showed the importance of believing the earliest words in Genesis, "in the beginning God". We spoke about God's ability to create. We noted at the point in time when God's government ruled the universe, and later, saw when God initiated the earth's government or that of humankind. Additionally, we mentioned God's sovereignty.

While we did not mention it at the time, it is imperative to realize that while God is sovereign, He delegated authority to humankind's government with accountability to Him. As humankind functions within their governmental mantle, with the choice to either rule in righteousness or not, that does not remove God's sovereignty.

In many places in scripture, we see where God overruled earth's government to spare His righteous. For example, Daniel in the lion's den, condemned to death for a crime he did not commit. God stopped the mouth of the lions[36]. Also, the three men thrown into the fiery furnace for holding the law of God regarding idolatry. Not willing to bow their knees to the idol of gold made by Nebuchadnezzar, they were sentenced to death. Yet, God intervened and stopped the flames from harming them[37].

God's government is, was and always will be, greater than any government upon the earth and His sovereignty still reigns. Perhaps, people do not always make a plea to God for help, or perhaps God's choice is not to intervene. Nevertheless, the point is that He can and often does, and that every earth's government gives account to Him.

---

[36] *Daniel 6: 7-24;*
[37] *Daniel 3:1-30*

Chapter 6
Themes Conclusion

Regarding Theme # 1, we saw God as a Father to all nations, and as a merciful redeemer. This led us into theme # 2, Redemption. Before reviewing Redemption's theme, please note that regarding Theme # 1, there are many areas we did not cover, such as revelation of His names, which further define God's character. Additionally, there are areas that describe the Godhead, and how the Godhead functions. These are branches which stream from the root of the fact that God is.

THEME # 2: REDEMPTION
As we discussed this theme, we spoke of the accountability of all humankind to YeHoVaH, including anyone who rules over another, whether that person is a parent, or an elder over a group, or a government official over a small area of nation. All give an account to the Almighty.

Additionally, we discussed the day of accountability, better known as the day of the LORD. We saw how this day comes to all and is prophetic to a final day of the LORD, a great and terrible day. The prophetic days of YHVH are not only rehearsals but are also characteristic of God's mercy as He calls all to repent and return to Him.

Bible Study Basics
A Closer Look at God's Word

As we studied the theme of the day of the LORD, we saw that the 7th day of creation never ended. We noted that the term often referred to regarding that day is this age. Similarly, we noted that the promised restoration comes at the end of day 7, or at the end of the age. Then comes the millennium reign of Yeshua, followed by a new[38] heaven and earth.

Lastly, we noted that the event that divides or separates day 7 from restoration is the Day of the Lord.

Dear Reader:
Keeping these two major themes in mind as you proceed to understand the Bible, will keep the Bible in context as you study it. In keeping Theme # 1 alive in your mind, the fact that God is, you should receive insight as you recognize God's sovereign ability as He moves towards humankind, and as He establishes prophetic pictures within the First Covenant and reveals them in the New.

Surely, the message of the prophets should come alive as Theme # 1 gives you insight as to the unfolding message of God as redeemer, even showing the revelation of Messiah through the first covenant.

---

[38] New or renewed.

Chapter 6
Themes Conclusion

John 5:39
> *"Search the scriptures; for in them ye think ye have eternal life: and they are they which testify of me."*

As you remember Theme # 2, the redemption theme, you should see that theme running from Genesis to the end of the book of Revelation, showing it as one continuous theme on the heart of God regarding humankind.

Keeping that theme in mind helps you to recognize the message of God calling all humankind, including Israel and other nations, into accountability through the prophets. Above all, as your spiritual eyes see God, you should recognize God's love, compassion, and mercy as He employs great measures to call people to repent and turn to Him.

Truly it is as Peter said:

2 Peter 3:9
> *"The Lord is not slack concerning his promise, as some men count slackness; but is longsuffering to us-ward, not willing that any should perish, but that all should come to repentance."*

Indeed, we have a great and powerful God.

Bible Study Basics
A Closer Look at God's Word

Psalm 147:5
"Great is our Lord, and of great power: his understanding is infinite."

Psalm 136:1-8
*"**1** O give thanks unto YHVH; for he is good: for his mercy endureth for ever. **2** O give thanks unto the God of gods: for his mercy endureth for ever. **3** O give thanks to the Lord of lords: for his mercy endureth for ever. **4** To him who alone doeth great wonders: for his mercy endureth for ever. **5** To him that by wisdom made the heavens: for his mercy endureth for ever. **6** To him that stretched out the earth above the waters: for his mercy endureth for ever. **7** To him that made great lights: for his mercy endureth for ever: **8** The sun to rule by day: for his mercy endureth for ever:"*

REMEMBER THESE TWO THEMES:

God Is and Redemption.

Never forget the day of accountability, either! As you explore Bible passages, see those passages in their position within the overall message of the Bible, within the whole counsel of God. In that way, whether you study prophecy, end times, or various other themes within the Word, your conclusions should have balance, and your application of the Word more effective. In short, remembering these things helps to keep you, the student, walking on safe ground.

COURSE 104
Bible Study Basics Continued

SECTION 3

Discovering Its Contents

CHAPTER 7

LEARNING ITS STRUCTURE

"I will delight myself in thy statutes: I will not forget thy word."

Psalm 119:16

A BIBLE TODAY CONTAINS 66 books, divided into two major sections, which the Bible describes:

Hebrews 8:7
"For if that first covenant had been faultless, then should no place have been sought for the second."

Here the author commenting on the new for two covenants, begins to offer an explanation, but in doing so, also, gives us the major sections:

1. First Covenant, often referred to as the Old Covenant, which contains 39 books.

2. Second Covenant, often referred to as the New Covenant, which contains 27 books.

The books in their canonical order are as follows:

BIBLE STRUCTURE[39]:

FIRST COVENANT	
1.	Genesis
2.	Exodus
3.	Leviticus
4.	Numbers
5.	Deuteronomy
6.	Joshua
7.	Judges
8.	Ruth
9.	1 Samuel
10.	2 Samuel
11.	1 Kings
12.	2 Kings
13.	1 Chronicles
14.	2 Chronicles
15.	Ezra
16.	Nehemiah
17.	Esther

---

[39] Roman Catholics add another 72 books, (73 if Lamentations is separate from Jeremiah, who wrote it.)

Chapter 7
Learning Its Structure

18.	Job
19.	Psalms
20.	Proverbs
21.	Ecclesiastes
22.	Song of Solomon
23.	Isaiah
24.	Jeremiah
25.	Lamentations
26.	Ezekiel
27.	Daniel
28.	Hosea
29.	Joel
30.	Amos
31.	Obadiah
32.	Jonah
33.	Micah
34.	Nahum
35.	Habakkuk
36.	Zephaniah
37.	Haggai
38.	Zechariah
39.	Malachi

SECOND COVENANT

1.	Matthew
2.	Mark
3.	Luke
4.	John

5.	Acts
6.	Romans
7.	1 Corinthians
8.	2 Corinthians
9.	Galatians
10.	Ephesians
11.	Philippians
12.	Colossians
13.	1 Thessalonians
14.	2 Thessalonians
15.	1 Timothy
16.	2 Timothy
17.	Titus
18.	Philemon
19.	Hebrews
20.	James
21.	1 Peter
22.	2 Peter
23.	1 John
24.	2 John
25.	3 John
26.	Jude
27.	Revelation

TANUK STRUCTURE

The Hebrew Tanuk is an anacronym. Taking the first letter in each section, namely, **T**orah, **N**ev'im and **K**etuvim, they arrive at the word TaNuK). The Torah

Chapter 7
Learning Its Structure

holds the five books of Moses; the Nev'im the prophets and the Ketuvim, the writings.

The books in their Hebrew order are as follows:

TORAH	NEVI'IM	KETUVIM
Moses 5 books	**Prophets**	**Writings**
Bereshit	Yehoshua	Tehillim
(Genesis)	(Joshua)	(Psalms)
Shamet	Shoftim	Mishlei
(Exodus)	(Judges)	(Proverbs)
Vayikra	Shmuel 1	Iyov
(Leviticus)	(1 Samuel)	(Job)
Bamidbar	Shmuel 2	Shir Hashirim
(Numbers)	(2nd Samuel)	(Song of Songs)
Devarim	Melachim	Rut
(Deuteronomy)	(1 Kings)	(Ruth)
	Melachim	Eichah
	(2 Kings)	(Lamentations)
	Yeshayahu	Kohelet
	(Isaiah)	(Ecclesiastes)
	Yirmiyahu	Esther
	(Jeremiah)	
	Yechezkel	Daniel
	(Ezekiel)	
	Hoshea	Ezra
	(Hosea)	
	Yoel	Nechemiah

(Joel)	(Nehamiah)
Amos	Divrei Hayamim 1
	1 Chronicles
Ovadiah	Divrei Hayamim 2
(Obadiah)	2 Chronicles
Yonah	
(Jonah)	
Micah	
(Micah)	
Nachum	
(Nahum)	
Chavakuk	
(Habakkuk)	
Tzefaniah	
(Zephaniah)	
Chaggai	
(Haggai)	
Zechariah	
Malachi	

Note: They divide the Nevi'im (Prophets) into two groups:
- **Former Prophets**, which are Joshua, Judges, Samuel, Kings.

Chapter 7
Learning Its Structure

- ***Latter Prophets***, which are Isaiah, Jeremiah, and Ezekiel, plus twelve minor prophets[40].[41]

TORAH/LAW DIFFERENCE

In the Christian Bible, the First Covenant includes the first 5 books of Moses, which some call the Pentateuch, or the Law. However, some Christians, in error, consider the entire First Covenant as the Law, and thus they likewise assume the whole First Covenant is the Torah. Torah means instruction, however, in the Hebrew picture language, its expanded meaning is interesting.

	TORAH	Strong's 8451	תּוֹרָה
ת	tov	Covenant, sign, last	
ו	vav	Nail, attach, fasten, join	
	Parent Root:	Fastened to a Covenant	
ר	resh	Head, above, highest	
ה	hey	Wonderful, awesome, breath (life), surrender	

---

[40] Minor prophet's term has nothing to do with the importance of the prophet but rather, their prophetic works were not as extensive as those of Isaiah, Jeremiah or Ezekiel.

[41] Note Daniel and the Psalms are not included in their prophetic books.

Child Root:	brings life, when surrendered, makes one the head
Overall meaning: Torah is a covenant, which when one attaches themselves to it, makes them the head, and brings life.	

Here we see that the picture language shows us the depth of what God's instructions bring to us when we bind ourselves or attach ourselves to following those instructions. As we surrender to those instructions, it makes us the head and brings forth life. That is what the Bible says:

Deuteronomy 28:13,
13 "And YHVH shall make thee the head, and not the tail; and thou shalt be above only, and thou shalt not be beneath; if that thou hearken unto the commandments of YHVH thy God, which I command thee this day, to observe and to do them:"

Proverbs 6:23
"For the commandment is a lamp; and the law is light; and reproofs of instruction are the way of life:"

Proverbs 4:20-22
"20 My son, attend to my words; incline thine ear unto my sayings. 21 Let them not depart from thine eyes; keep them in the midst of thine heart. 22 For they are life unto those that find them, and health to all their flesh."

Chapter 7
Learning Its Structure

Psalm 1:1-3

"1 ¶ Blessed is the man that walketh not in the counsel of the ungodly, nor standeth in the way of sinners, nor sitteth in the seat of the scornful. 2 But his delight is in the Torah[42] of YHVH; and in his Torah[43] doth he meditate day and night. 3 And he shall be like a tree planted by the rivers of water, that bringeth forth his fruit in his season; his leaf also shall not wither; and whatsoever he doeth shall prosper."

A NEW COVENANT REALITY

It is imperative that we understand one important fact about the New Covenant, otherwise, it will affect the way we interpret scripture. It depends on our understanding of the word, "New".

Jeremiah 31:31

"Behold, the days come, saith YHVH, that I will make a new covenant with the house of Israel, and with the house of Judah:"

Jeremiah, the prophet, related this word to Israel prior to their dispersal to Babylon. The word used for "new" is well worth considering.

---

[42] KJV interprets Strong's #8451 as Law.
[43] KJV interprets Strong's #8451 as Law.

Word	Strong's #44	Hebrew Word Used
New	2319 (root 2318) חָדָשׁ	חָדָשׁ chadash

This same **root word** for "new moon", is used in Hebrew.

Psalm 81:3
"Blow up the trumpet in the new moon, in the time appointed, on our solemn feast day."

Word	Strong's #45	Hebrew Word Used
New	2320 (root 2318) חָדָשׁ	חָדָשׁ chadash

Let's look at the moon:
"The moon goes through a cycle of eight phases, which repeat every 29.5 days:
- **New Moon**: the moon's unilluminated side faces the earth, so the moon is not visible.

---

[44] All references to Strong's in this work come from Online Bible Edition program, available for free on the internet.
[45] All references to Strong's in this work come from Online Bible Edition program, available for free on the internet.

- **Waxing Crescent**: a thin crescent of light is visible on the right side of the moon in the Northern Hemisphere.
- **First Quarter**: half the moon illuminated.
- **Waxing Gibbous**: the moon is more than half but not fully illuminated.
- **Full Moon**: the moon is completely illuminated.
- **Waning Gibbous**: the moon is between a full and a half moon.
- **Third Quarter**: half of the moon is illuminated, but on the opposite side as in the first quarter.
- **Waning Crescent**: a thin crescent of light is visible on the left side of the moon in the Northern Hemisphere."

"The moon's phases are caused by the relative positions of the moon and sun in the sky. The term "waxing" refers to a growing image of the moon, while "waning" refers to a shrinking image."

"The moon orbits Earth in about 27.3 days, but it takes about 29.5 days to go from one new moon to the next because of how sunlight hits the moon. The exact dates of full moons can vary depending on time zones and observing locations."

"The moon also rotates on its axis once every 27.3 days, which matches the time it takes to revolve around

Earth. This means that Earth observers always see the same side of the moon, called the "nearside".[46]

When the moon is seen every month, is it a different moon? Obviously, not! So why use the same word for "new moon" for the word translated as "new" regarding the covenant promised in Jeremiah 31:31?

While the concordance and others declare it means, brand new, it obviously does not suggest that God creates a new month every month. Rather, the intended meaning is different than brand new, meaning never seen before. To be accurate, "renewed" would be a better word than "new". That word implies it has undergone a change, *a renewal*, its cycle complete.

Taking this thought forward, and remembering Jeremiah used the same word for "new" covenant, could it mean "renewed"?

Jeremiah 31:31-34
*"**31** Behold, the days come, saith YHVH, that I will make a new covenant with the house of Israel, and with the house of Judah: **32** Not according to the covenant*

---

[46] All within quotation marks here are quotes from Google information, AI generative, search, cycles of the moon.

Chapter 7
Learning Its Structure

that I made with their fathers in the day that I took them by the hand to bring them out of the land of Egypt; which my covenant they brake, although I was an husband unto them, saith YHVH: 33 But this shall be the covenant that I will make with the house of Israel; After those days, saith YHVH, I will put my law **(8451 torah)** *in their inward parts, and write it in their hearts; and will be their God, and they shall be my people. 34 And they shall teach no more every man his neighbour, and every man his brother, saying, Know YHVH: for they shall all know me, from the least of them unto the greatest of them, saith YHVH: for I will forgive their iniquity, and I will remember their sin no more."*

This promised covenant reflects on a difference, here, for in that First Covenant, God's finger wrote on tablets of stone. However, in this promised covenant, God promised to write His Torah on the people's heart. Note, that in this passage, God did **not** promise to write an entire new set of laws! Rather, the same ones He wrote earlier, He would write on the hearts of His people. Therefore, in that God writes the same commandments only on hearts instead of stone, the promised covenant could be interpreted as renewed, due to its engravement on a different medium.

To reiterate, in the renewed covenant, God's writing finger exchanged the earlier tablets of stone for a newer format, writing on a person's heart. Furthermore, there is no hint, either, that God planned to alter those commandments. In fact, Yeshua affirmed God's commandments when He summed them up:

Matthew 22:37-40
*"**37** Jesus said unto him, Thou shalt love the Lord thy God with all thy heart, and with all thy soul, and with all thy mind. **38** This is the first and great commandment. **39** And the second is like unto it, Thou shalt love thy neighbour as thyself. **40** On these two commandments hang all the law and the prophets."*

Considering all these things, Jeremiah 31:31 could easily read,

Jeremiah 31:31
*"Behold, the days come, saith YHVH, that I will make a **renewed** covenant with the house of Israel, and with the house of Judah:"*

Therefore, as one looks at the First Covenant, one recognizes a continuation of that covenant in the Renewed Covenant. Furthermore, that continuation shows up in *the improved behaviour* of God's people, for He writes His Torah in their hearts, thus, in the

Chapter 7
Learning Its Structure

Renewed Covenant, people's behaviour should far outshine First Covenant people regarding the love they have for God and for each other. Yeshua certainly expects His followers to love Him, with all their being, as we saw in an earlier text[47], and extend their love towards others, which Yeshua reaffirmed in this passage below.

John 13:35
> *"By this shall all men know that ye are my disciples, if ye have love one to another."*

---

[47] Matthew 22:37-40

CHAPTER 8

GRASPING ITS PRECEPTS

"For precept must be upon precept, precept upon precept; line upon line, line upon line; here a little, and there a little:"

Isaiah 28:10 a)

WHEN LEARNING HOW to study the Bible, it is good to recognize that the Bible has many books, as seen in the last chapter. Additionally, each book, while fitting in with the overall themes of the Bible, also has a unique purpose. Discovering that purpose helps one in the interpretation of the book.

Within each book, while the author had an intended purpose, many other truths lay within that book. One such book, rich in many truths, is the book of Isaiah. Isaiah, speaking to a stubborn, rebellious people, calling them to repent, said this about God's Word:

Isaiah 28:9-13
> "9 ¶ *Whom shall he teach knowledge? and whom shall he make to understand doctrine? [them that are] weaned from the milk, [and] drawn from the breasts. 10 For precept [must be] upon precept, precept upon precept; line upon line, line upon line; here a little, [and] there a little: 11 For with stammering lips and another tongue will he speak to this people. 12 To whom he said, This [is] the rest [wherewith] ye may cause the weary to rest; and this [is] the refreshing: yet they would not hear. 13 But the word of YHVH was unto them precept upon precept, precept upon precept; line upon line, line upon line; here a little, [and] there a little; that they might go, and fall backward, and be broken, and snared, and taken.*"

Here, Isaiah asks two questions, to which he answers.
1. To whom shall he teach knowledge?
2. To whom shall he make to understand doctrine?

Consider the fact that Isaiah spoke to a Jewish audience. If the temple priests of their day properly performed their tasks, then those within Judeah should know the very things Isaiah taught them. What he taught them was not hard, yet the people did not understand.

Chapter 8
Grasping Its Precepts

He explains to them, that even babes just weaned from breast feeding could get the principles, for "precept upon precept, line upon line" one learns. Here a little, and there a little". In other words, take a precept, which is a principle, a scriptural instruction, and piece it together with other principles, learning about the things of God, one step at a time.

Isaiah then tells them of their stubbornness and refusal to learn. If they had learned, then rest and refreshment would be the result. However, they refused to hear. He then repeats the simplicity of the Word, explaining again that it can be grasped, precept upon precept, line upon line, here a little and there a little.

Following this reminder, Isaiah makes a powerful statement, "that they might go, and fall backward, and be broken and snared and taken". To understand this saying, first read Isaiah 29:13:

Isaiah 29:13
"Wherefore the Lord said, Forasmuch as this people draw near me with their mouth, and with their lips do honour me, but have removed their heart far from me, and their fear toward me is taught by the precept of men:"

Here stands the root cause for their inability to hear:

They honoured God with only their mouth, but their hearts were far from Him. These people refused to love their God with all their heart, mind, soul and strength as admonished in the Word. Instead, they ignored His precepts, the result of which is the use of human wisdom. That will never bring a person to know God. One needs Godly wisdom to know God. That wisdom comes from knowing His Precepts.

Also, if it is precept upon precept, and line upon line, it is not an instant knowing. It takes time. It takes effort. It takes dedication. This lesson, Yeshua taught:

Matthew 13:45-46
> "**45** *Again, the kingdom of heaven is like unto a merchant man, seeking goodly pearls:* **46** *Who, when he had found one pearl of great price, went and sold all that he had, and bought it."*

Put in simple terms, to understand the things of God, is like this:

A merchant, a person who travels looking to build his fortune, found a precious thing. Seeing it of great value, he sold everything that he owned just to buy it. In other words, he saw its value so great, that all he earned and worked for all his life was nothing

Chapter 8
Grasping Its Precepts

compared to the value of what he found. Therefore, he sold everything just to own that special treasure.

Such is the way with the things of God. One must perceive God as the greatest treasure on the earth. Additionally, one must treasure the same things that God treasures, such as His Word for it contains the precepts of God.

Knowing those precepts, one by one, we build our knowledge of God, but at its core, the fire of God burns within to know Him and His ways. Such did Joshua and he advised Israel to do the same:

Joshua 22:5
> *"But take diligent heed to do the commandment and the law, which Moses the servant of YHVH charged you, to love YHVH your God, and to walk in all his ways, and to keep his commandments, and to cleave unto him, and to serve him with all your heart and with all your soul."*

In this passage we hear of obeying the Word of the Lord, to love God, walk in His Ways, keep His commandments, and cleave[48] or cling unto Him, and to serve Him with all your being. This brings us to the

---

[48] To cleave means to attach yourself to Him to be one with Him!

point of this chapter, the reason for Bible Study: to learn to know God.

LEARNING TO KNOW GOD
From that passage in Isaiah, we see good reason to learn the Word of God, remembering to honour God with a correct heart in the matter so that we know God inwardly, not just honour Him outwardly. Other passages in the Word, too, tell us about learning about God.

Psalm 119:1-5
1 ALEPH. Blessed are the undefiled in the way, who walk in the law of YHVH. 2 Blessed are they that keep his testimonies, and that seek him with the whole heart. 3 They also do no iniquity: they walk in his ways."

"4 ¶ Thou hast commanded us to keep thy precepts diligently. 5 O that my ways were directed to keep thy statutes!"

In this Psalm, we hear a reinforcement of what we learned earlier about walking with God, keeping His Torah (instructions), His testimonies, and seeking Him with the whole heart. In this passage we also see what seeking God with our whole heart brings, "to walk in His ways", and thus, not lead a sinful life.

Chapter 8
Grasping Its Precepts

Psalm 119 goes on to remind the listener, to keep God's precepts, *with diligence*. Then the Psalmist excitedly exclaims, "O, that my ways were directed to keep thy statutes!"

Our Psalmist continues:

Psalm 119:6-11
> "6 Then shall I not be ashamed, when I have respect unto all thy commandments. 7 I will praise thee with uprightness of heart, when I shall have learned thy righteous judgments. 8 I will keep thy statutes: O forsake me not utterly."

> "9 ¶ BETH. Wherewithal shall a young man cleanse his way? by taking heed [thereto] according to thy word. 10 With my whole heart have I sought thee: O let me not wander from thy commandments. 11 ¶ Thy word have I hid in mine heart, that I might not sin against thee."

Then, says the Psalmist, I shall not be ashamed, when I have respect, or give deep regard to all God's commandments. He then speaks of some of the other benefits for treasuring God and His Word. He will praise God with an upright heart, or a heart is right by learning and doing God's ways. When he has learned God's righteous judgments, he will keep God's statutes.

As the Psalmist from 119 continues, he points back to the youth and asks how God's precepts could benefit them. Specifically, he says, how shall a young man cleanse his ways? Then, he answers the question, emphatically, by declaring, by taking heed or listening to the things taught in God's Word.

He, then, reiterates, that he sought God with his whole heart, pleading with God not to let him wander from His commandments. He shares the steps he took towards those ends, too, as he says, Your Word I hid in my heart. He treasured it, kept it close before Him, purposely, so he would not sin, and offend God.

Indeed, this Psalmist knew truth for centuries later, Yeshua reaffirmed the importance of keeping watch over one's heart.

Mark 7:18-23
*"**18** And he saith unto them, Are ye so without understanding also? Do ye not perceive, that whatsoever thing from without entereth into the man, it cannot defile him; 19 Because it entereth not into his heart, but into the belly, and goeth out into the draught, purging all meats? 20 And he said, That which cometh out of the man, that defileth the man. 21 For from within, out of the heart of men, proceed evil thoughts,*

adulteries, fornications, murders, 22 Thefts, covetousness, wickedness, deceit, lasciviousness, an evil eye, blasphemy, pride, foolishness: 23 All these evil things come from within, and defile the man."

Yeshua taught it well, for the heart in Hebraic, Biblical thinking, shows the heart as the place from where sin originates. Therefore, it is good to do what Psalm 119 advises as well as what the writer of Proverbs, King Solomon, recommends:

Proverbs 4:23
"Keep thy heart with all diligence; for out of it are the issues of life."

Yeshua, Solomon, as well as the writer of Psalm 119 knew, the centre of concern is the heart. Looking back to Isaiah's words, in Isaiah 29:13, the people drew near to God with their mouth, but their heart was far from Him.

To keep one's heart is sound wisdom, especially then it comes from a fire of love burning deep within. Such a heart reveals a person who desperately wants to know God and know His ways. Such a person leans into the task with all their being, so as not to disappoint the God they so love.

Psalm 119:12-16
*"**12** Blessed art thou, O LORD: teach me thy statutes. **13** ¶ With my lips have I declared all the judgments of thy mouth. **14** I have rejoiced in the way of thy testimonies, as much as in all riches. **15** I will meditate in thy precepts, and have respect unto thy ways. **16** I will delight myself in thy statutes: I will not forget thy word."*

In the Psalmist's passion to serve God in ways that please God, he asks God to teach him His statutes, as he wants to learn direct from God. Then, he says that his lips have declared or spoken aloud, the judgments that came from God's mouth. He rejoiced as he went about doing the things God desired, treasuring them like riches. He mediates, continually bringing God's precepts and one more time, speaks about how he gives regard to God's ways. He thoroughly delights in God's statutes, and he promises never to forget God's Word.

Truly, this Psalmist is an excellent example for all who wish to know God and His ways. His study was not a flippant study, but rather came from a desire to know God, His Ways, and how to please God. Surely, this Psalmist's example in learning inspires one, too, for he diligently sought God for His guidance, giving respect to His ways.

Chapter 8
Grasping Its Precepts

GLEANINGS FROM THIS CHAPTER
When a person decides to know God, their commitment absolutely must come from deep within, shifting past the initial grasp of the mind. It needs to burn like a fire deep within the heart. Likewise, learning about God, stems from that same place. It is, therefore, in one's heart that a determination grows so that from day one of meeting God through that born-again[49] experience, to the rest of their life, they draw near to God.

Walking this way, pressing in through the Word, prayer, and worship, as one's life unfolds, they develop a priceless relationship. With the help of the Holy Spirit guarding their heart, they seize the opportunity to learn how to be a friend of God, as that is what God called one of His most trusted and valued servants:

> 2 Chronicles 20:7
> *"Art not thou our God, who didst drive out the inhabitants of this land before thy people Israel, and gavest it to the seed of Abraham thy friend for ever?"*

Also, this friendship, James the Apostle, reiterated:

---

[49] A term used to mean one who accepted Messiah through the message of salvation. For that message, read the Message of Salvation in the Appendix.

James 2:23
"And the scripture was fulfilled which saith, Abraham believed God, and it was imputed unto him for righteousness: and he was called the Friend of God."

This is the bottom line in learning the Word of God. This is the Pearl of great price of which Yeshua spoke. He is the reason why one takes the time to get into the Word!

***

Dear Reader:

With these chapters laid out before you, if you embrace the principles presented to you from the beginning unto now, you should do well employing the actual practical steps of learning the Word in the next section.

Bible Study Basics

SECTION 4

Discovering Its Truths

In this section, you will learn some basics study techniques. Techniques are mechanical, so it is important, before you learn these techniques, that you aim to embrace the principles already discussed in this book. To do so, brings a lifeline to a lifetime of learning with the bottom line of a relationship with God.

CHAPTER 9

BIBLE STUDY WISDOM

"I have chosen the way of truth: thy judgments have I laid before me."

Psalm 119:30

HERE, WE WILL PICK UP a theme from our introduction about the Word of God. It is not only truth, but it is a living truth. So, when studying any passage of the Bible, as one opens it, remember it is a living word, therefore, no matter what part you read, it has a job to do, and it will do that job.

Hebrews 4:12
"For the word of God is quick (living), and powerful, and sharper than any two-edged sword, piercing even to the dividing asunder of soul and spirit, and of the joints and marrow, and is a discerner of the thoughts and intents of the heart."

A Closer Look at God's Word

When dealing with God's Word, expect the Word to speak to you. In other words, believe that the portion of text you read will come alive to you. This helps you approach the Word of God in faith.

> *Hebrews 11:6*
> *"But without faith it is impossible to please him: for he that cometh to God must believe that he is, and that he is a rewarder of them that diligently seek him."*

As you open the Word of God, do so with this thought in mind, "I am coming to God, believing that He exists, and He will show me marvellous things out of His Word[50]."

TO STUDY THE WORD OF GOD

According to the King James Version, there are only three passages where it uses the English word, *study*.

> *Ecclesiastes 12:9-12*
> *"**9** And moreover, because the preacher was wise, he still taught the people knowledge; yea, he gave good heed, and sought out, and set in order many proverbs.*
> ***10** The preacher sought to find out acceptable words:*

---

[50] Psalm 119:18 *"Open thou mine eyes, that I may behold wondrous things out of thy law."*

and that which was written was upright, even words of truth. **11** *The words of the wise are as goads, and as nails fastened by the masters of assemblies, which are given from one shepherd.* **12** *And further, by these, my son, be admonished: of making many books there is no end; and much study <03854> is a weariness of the flesh.*

Word	Strong's #	Hebrew Word Used
study	3854	לַהַג *lah'-hag*
It comes from an unused root meaning to be eager, interpreted as study, devotion to study.		

In this passage which uses this Hebrew word, the admonition speaks of a preacher who was wise. In his wisdom he taught the people knowledge, calling them to pay attention to the lessons of life they needed to hear.

Additionally, with a warning in mind, he searched out and presented many truths to his listeners. He sought to find words that were acceptable to God, from that which had already been written and considered righteous. In other words, what the scriptures taught, he considered as the whole counsel of God and gave that truth to his listeners, sparing nothing.

Solomon, the author, continues to speak of the value of such words. He says the words of the wise of as goads. A goad is an ancient tool used to probe oxen or cattle in the direction that they need to go. There is a suggestion here that words of wisdom, like a goad, might be resisted, but nevertheless people should listen to them because they will lead us to a much better place, when heeded.

These sayings or teaching prepared and presented by the wise, come from leaders of the assemblies who are called by God to watch over the sheep. So, therefore, be admonished by these words but be careful of the words of others, of those who write books, just to write them. This infers to avoid that which is simply spouting off at the mouth.

So, the warning here, is to use discernment, both when listening as well as writing. Ensure the words spoken are sourced in God's wisdom and thus, they will contain truth. Unless they do, studying them will only make one weary, with no benefit to the growth of true knowledge.

While this gives us some excellent insight into studying the Word, especially considering what we can expect from it and learn what we must do with our studies, there is another word in Hebrew which,

Chapter 9
Bible Study Wisdom

although not interpreted as study, nevertheless give us an idea of what God desires for His children. It is the following word:

Word	Strong's #	Hebrew Word Used
Seek	1875	דָּרַשׁ daw-rash'
Amongst its meanings are the words, seek, search, investigate and to study.		

Seeking YeHoVaH, searching for Him, investigating and studying Him produces good fruit: Here are a few places where KJV interpreted the word 1875, which expresses a good result:

Deuteronomy 4:29
  "But if from thence thou shalt seek YHVH thy God, thou shalt find him, if thou seek him with all thy heart and with all thy soul."

Psalm 53:2
  "God looked down from heaven upon the children of men, to see if there were any that did understand, that did seek God."

Isaiah 55:6
  "Seek ye YHVH while he may be found, call ye upon him while he is near:"

Hosea 10:12
"Sow to yourselves in righteousness, reap in mercy; break up your fallow ground: for it is time to seek YHVH, till he come and rain righteousness upon you."

Moving on to the passages in the New Covenant, in both places the word aligns closer to what we consider to study:

1 Thessalonians 4:11-12
"11 And that ye study to be quiet, and to do your own business, and to work with your own hands, as we commanded you; 12 That ye may walk honestly toward them that are without, and that ye may have lack of nothing."

2 Timothy 2:15
"Study to shew thyself approved unto God, a workman that needeth not to be ashamed, rightly dividing the word of truth."

In the first scripture, the author, Paul, advises the believers to study to be quiet, to do their own business, to walk honestly with people outside of the religious community[51], and to ensure they had no lack. In today's language Paul gives the believers wisdom on how to function in the world around them, being at

---

[51] It was understood that they were at peace with those within their own assembly.

Chapter 9
Bible Study Wisdom

peace with all people, earning a living, providing for themselves and ensuring they kept their own households.

Simply put, all who could take the responsibility of caring for themselves should do so. That action released the assembly of believers to care for those who were not capable of providing for themselves.

In the latter scripture, we find two very important concepts which Paul stressed for believers. First, one should study the scripture for the approval of God. Second, Paul strongly suggests that we present the truth for what it is, not looking for the approval of others. In other words, speak but not to tickle people's ears!

> *2 Timothy 4:1-4*
> *"**1** I charge thee therefore before God, and the Lord Jesus Christ, who shall judge the quick and the dead at his appearing and his kingdom; **2** Preach the word; be instant in season, out of season; reprove, rebuke, exhort with all longsuffering and doctrine. **3** For the time will come when they will not endure sound doctrine; but after their own lusts shall they heap to themselves teachers, having itching ears; **4** And they shall turn away their ears from the truth, and shall be turned unto fables."*

In days like this that the apostle, Paul, described, those who present the Word must keep their eyes on God. In doing so, they will preach the Word and with the same vigour whether it is wanted, (in season) or it is not wanted (out of season).

Using the Word to reprove, rebuke or exhort, and doing so with patience and doctrine, meaning not to adjust it to fit the desires of those listening, as verse 3 advises. That is truly out of season, for a time is coming (and perhaps is now here) when people will not heap teachers to themselves who tell them what they want to hear, having turned their eyes away from truth and instead cling to lies, even fables.

Finally, in 2 Timothy 2:15, Paul admonished believers to rightly divide the Word of God, or in modern words, keep the Word in context. In other words, all insights, theories, or discussions on the Word, based on the Word, must be truly sourced in the Word. All presented and taught come with righteousness with no vain motives. The teachings originate from an upright heart.

Here are a few basic reminders to use as one moves forward to learn the Word.

Chapter 9
Bible Study Wisdom

REMEMBER: IT IS GOD'S WORD

Take time when reading the Word of God, looking at it prayerfully and carefully. After all, it is the Word of the Supreme Being of all heaven and earth.

Habakkuk 2:20
   "But YHVH is in his holy temple: let all the earth keep silence before him."

REMEMBER: GOD'S WORD IS AUTHORITATIVE

As the written Word of God came to us through God's selected or chosen vessels, as the Holy Spirit inspired them, give way to God's authority[52].

2 Timothy 3:16
   "All scripture is given by inspiration of God, and is profitable for doctrine, for reproof, for correction, for instruction in righteousness."

Also, in today's world, in some circles, certain people elevate a modern, current prophetic word as either equal or, unfortunately at times, greater than the Word of God. God's Word, in its original language has authority, and His written word takes precedence over every word spoken by modern day prophets, no matter how divinely inspired that prophet appears to

---

[52] Here, make a distinction: *God's Word, as it was written, in its original language, and in the context wherein it was given has authority.*

be. God never changes, neither does His written Word[53].

REMEMBER, GOD'S WORD IS LIVING

If one approaches the Word of God as a living entity, giving it the respect it is due, then one prepares their heart to receive its message.

> *John 6:63*
> *"It is the spirit that quickeneth; the flesh profiteth nothing: the words that I speak unto you, they are spirit, and they are life."*

REMEMBER: THE GOAL

It is so easy to become wrapped up in the art of learning, including the study of God's Word. Students of the Word must never lose focus on the goal. It is not to obtain knowledge only! It is, rather, to know God and His Ways. Also, the study of the Word of God offers the student opportunity to become more like the subject of which they studied. In other words, as a student of God's Word, give room for Holy Spirit lessons, giving opportunity for God's character to come alive, even enough to change you!

---

[53] Our understanding of His written Word might change as we grow in our grasp of God, but His written Word does not change.

CHAPTER 10

BIBLE STUDY TECHNIQUES

"But the word [is] very nigh unto thee, in thy mouth, and in thy heart, that thou mayest do it."

Deuteronomy 30:14

WHEN MOVING FORWARD to study God's Word, it becomes imperative to realize that any person, with a sincere heart, can learn the Word of God. Even in the First Covenant, many passages declare the knowing God and His Word is possible. Like this one in our opening scripture, which states, God's Word is very near to you, and in your heart that you might do it.

Prophets like Isaiah, also spoke of the ability to grasp the concepts in God's Word. Gleaning this ability is the first step in the techniques of learning God's Word:

Isaiah 48:17-19
"17 Thus saith YHVH, thy Redeemer, the Holy One of Israel; I [am] YHVH thy God which teacheth thee to profit, which leadeth thee by the way [that] thou shouldest go. 18 O that thou hadst hearkened to my commandments! then had thy peace been as a river, and thy righteousness as the waves of the sea: 19 Thy seed also had been as the sand, and the offspring of thy bowels like the gravel thereof; his name should not have been cut off nor destroyed from before me."

Verse 17 declares that YeHoVaH, the Redeemer, the Holy One of Israel is YeHoVaH, your God, which teaches you by the way where you should go. Here, God promises to teach His own. Then, He continues to reminisce with His people, looking at what could have been if only they would have listened to His commandments. Note a promise for Israel regarding peace, for Israel's peace would run like a river, and their righteousness as the waves of the sea. Also, their seed would have been so great in number, more numerous than the sand, and their offspring like gravel. Then, even their name, God would honour.

Isaiah 54:11-14
"11 ¶ O thou afflicted, tossed with tempest, [and] not comforted, behold, I will lay thy stones with fair

Chapter 10
Bible Study Techniques

colours, and lay thy foundations with sapphires. 12 And I will make thy windows of agates, and thy gates of carbuncles, and all thy borders of pleasant stones. 13 And all thy children [shall be] taught of YHVH; and great [shall be] the peace of thy children. 14 In righteousness shalt thou be established: thou shalt be far from oppression; for thou shalt not fear: and from terror; for it shall not come near thee."

Speaking into a promised time of restoration, God's compassion reaches out towards His People. They were tossed, afflicted with a tempest, a deep and powerful wind, and not comforted. God promises to restore them, laying their stones with beautiful colours, and foundations with sapphires, a precious jewel.

He speaks of making their windows of agates, and their gates of carbuncles, more precious stones. Then He proclaims that all of their children shall be taught of YeHoVaH, and note again, the promise of peace with these words, "great shall be the peace of thy children".

He continues with the promise of His restoration of Israel, which shall be established in righteousness, and Israel shall be far from oppression, and terror.

Moving on into the New Covenant, we have such passages as from the gospel of John:

> *John 14:25-27*
> *"25 ¶ These things have I spoken unto you, being yet present with you. 26 But the Comforter, which is the Holy Ghost, whom the Father will send in my name, he shall teach you all things, and bring all things to your remembrance, whatsoever I have said unto you. 27 Peace I leave with you, my peace I give unto you: not as the world giveth, give I unto you. Let not your heart be troubled, neither let it be afraid."*

Here, Yeshua speaks to His Disciples about the coming of the Comforter, the Holy Spirit, Whom the Father sends in His Name. He, the Holy Spirit, shall teach you all things, and bring things to your remembrance whatsoever Yeshua said. Note again, the connection to peace!

In Colossians, this theme of peace also connects with the Word:

> *Colossians 3:15-16*
> *"15 And let the peace of God rule in your hearts, to the which also ye are called in one body; and be ye thankful. 16 Let the word of Christ dwell in you*

Chapter 10
Bible Study Techniques

richly in all wisdom; teaching and admonishing one another in psalms and hymns and spiritual songs, singing with grace in your hearts to the Lord."

So many amazing benefits come to believers as they pursue to know the Lord and His Word! Even, promises of abilities to properly discern, awaits the one who has learned to abide in Him:

> 1 John 2:26-29
> "**26** *These things have I written unto you concerning them that seduce you.* **27** *But the anointing which ye have received of him abideth in you, and ye need not that any man teach you: but as the same anointing teacheth you of all things, and is truth, and is no lie, and even as it hath taught you, ye shall abide in him.* **28** ¶ *And now, little children, abide in him; that, when he shall appear, we may have confidence, and not be ashamed before him at his coming.* **29** *If ye know that he is righteous, ye know that every one that doeth righteousness is born of him."*

John the Apostle, knowing that deceptions are possible, and that not every teacher has pure motives, wrote of the necessity to abide in Yeshua. He prefaced that word by speaking of the anointing, referring to the

Holy Spirit, that teaches all things, and is truth and the One[54] in Whom we abide.

After speaking about the truest form of abiding, John speaks of Yeshua's coming. When He appears, there will be confidence and not shame, exclaiming that "if we know that He is righteous, then, we know that everyone born of Him does that same righteousness".

In learning to know God's Word, then, we first seek God for His Spirit to teach us. This is the first and most important step:

ASK FOR THE HOLY SPIRIT TO TEACH YOU!

Dear Reader, these following tips are intended to help you as much as possible, and therefore, the narrative is directed to you, rather than to all.

READ IT CAREFULLY
Because the Word of God is His Word, it is a valued treasure, therefore, reading it carefully and prayerfully brings a respect for it. Also, employing some reading habits is good. For example, when you read a book for the study of it, first read the book, without trying to interpret it. Read it for its connection to God, asking

---

[54] The Holy Spirit is the Spirit of Yeshua.

Chapter 10
Bible Study Techniques

Him for insight, yes, but do not make your first read your time of searching for content read.

When reading a book, read it repeatedly and while you're waiting on the Holy Spirit, listen to it continually, as often as possible. In this way, you prepare yourself to receive an impression about the overall content of the book. Later, when the Spirit begins to open your eyes to these scriptures, you will have put yourself on safe ground for the insight for which you sought Him.

KEEP IT IN CONTEXT
Integrity in life, especially when quoting another, means to reliably repeat what a person said, not twisting their words to our advantage or take its meaning out of context. If that integrity is important regarding another person's word, how much more when it comes to God's Word. Reading the book, repeatedly, as mentioned above, will help with keeping context. Also, as you read the book as a whole, you should look at its historical, geographical and instructional contents.

Historical Content
When reading a Bible book, grab hold of the timeframe of the book, *in the history of Israel*. It is during or after the exodus; or before or after the exile, and the like.

When you first read and listen to the book, listen for such details. Later, when you become familiar with the book, take some time and research historical evidence outside the Bible, such as a source which might verify time of the Kings, or certain prophets. Just remember, the Bible is the history of Israel!

Geographical Content
Israel went through many challenges in obtaining the Promised land. Understanding the geography of the land helps to make certain passages come alive, especially why some battles happened in certain places. Other significant sites might be so because of its position in the land, for example, a city on a well-established trade route might be a place of income for whoever owned it. Perhaps a certain portion of land might be agriculturally important due to certain water wells. A geographical understanding gives more insight into some Bible characters, as to why they did certain things, or even fought certain battles.

Instructional Content
As you search through the scriptures, you want to understand the Bible's instructions. It holds great information for understanding God's idea of righteousness, disciplines for living, goals and aspiration worth pursuing and the like. Remember, the word Torah means instruction, and within the five

Chapter 10
Bible Study Techniques

books of Moses you find detailed instructions on true life.

Other books in the Bible contain great wisdom, such as Proverbs. Discover worship in the Psalms, and enjoy their poetic and prophetic literature, too. Whatever book you read, experience their instructions for living and embrace them.

ABSORB ITS SURFACE MEANING, FIRST
While God's Word has a depth to it like none other word, its meaning when given is very important. It came through God's messenger with an original intent, and while it might have some far-reaching prophetic meaning, its original meaning must not be forgotten. As you read and listen to the Word, you might want to jot down on paper some things that spoke to you. Often, (but not always) they are good indicators to the direction where the Spirit desires to take you. Later, when studying, you can weigh them out carefully.

COME WITH A FRESH MINDSET
When approaching any book, even if you studied it previously, you want to approach it without a preconceived mindset. Always come with a humble heart and a desire to learn, or if necessary, unlearn! At times, many factors accidentally prejudice the mind. So, approach the subject with a desire for truth and

nothing but the truth, willing to shed any bias or former teachings which might contradict its true meaning.

KEEP CHAPTER AND VERSES INTACT
Of course, after you think you are ready to do so, begin to study each chapter, keeping it in context with the overall message of the book. Also, do the same thing with the verses, keep them in context with the chapter and the overall message of the book.

KEEP ITS DEEPER MEANING IN BALANCE
When looking for deeper meaning, it is important to recognize that scripture interprets scripture. Scripture within the book should verify your findings. Also, any principle, idea or teaching you discover, other scriptures will confirm your conclusions.

If you remember these few tips, you should enjoy countless hours of learning the most precious book in the world: *The Bible*. To help you even further, included in this book is a section called, Discovering Its Truths. That section presents a proven way to analyze the scriptures to glean truth from them. Mastering that skill takes time, but when you do master it, the meaning of books, chapters and verses increases dramatically! May God bless you as you learn it!

Bible Study Basics

SECTION 5

Discovering Chapter Analysis

*This textbook chapter presents **a general outline** of the procedure of doing a chapter analysis. However, to completely grasp a chapter analysis, we prefer to teach it hands on. That experience awaits in the accompanying workbook. It has an additional chapter entitled, "Doing the Chapter Analysis".*

CHAPTER 11

CHAPTER ANALYSIS BASICS

*"**12** Now we have received, not the spirit of the world, but the spirit which is of God; that we might know the things that are freely given to us of God. **13** Which things also we speak, not in the words which man's wisdom teacheth, but which the Holy Ghost teacheth; comparing spiritual things with spiritual. **14** But the natural man receiveth not the things of the Spirit of God: for they are foolishness unto him: neither can he know them, because they are spiritually discerned."*

1 Corinthians 2:12-14

WHENEVER ONE TRIES to discover the truths of scripture, it is imperative that we ensure a connection with the Holy Spirit as He teaches every believer, without exception. Paul, the apostle, reiterates that fact in our opening scripture.

Bible Study Basics
A Closer Look at God's Word

In this passage from his first letter to the Corinthians, Paul says in verse 12, *"now we have received, not the spirit of the world"*, meaning that believers have not received that spirit that draws one into the carnal, temporal things of the world that appeals to the flesh. Rather, Paul states emphatically, the Holy Spirit presents to believers the knowledge of what God gave us, freely. In other words, our inheritance and the things of God, the Spirit wishes to teach us.

Verse 13 reinforces the facts that the Holy Spirit teaches us and in doing so, compares spiritual things with spiritual things. He does not teach us wisdom sourced from the carnal or human mind.

Verse 14 brings forward the bottom line, one that a good student of the Word never forgets: *"the **natural** man **receives not** the things of the Spirit of God"*.

In other words, looking at scriptures to understand then with the carnal or natural mind does not profit the person, spiritually. To embrace the things of the Spirit, one needs to learn from God's Spirit. Paul goes on to say that such things as taught by the carnal or human mind perceives the things of God as foolishness, or in today's world, it sees them as stupid, ridiculous, or unrealistic. Paul concludes his comments by reminding believers that to understand spiritual truths, they must discern or discover them spiritually, through the help of the Holy Spirit.

Bottom line:
The natural or carnal mind understands natural things. It cannot grasp God's spiritual truths.

The spiritual mind understands spiritual things. Through the Holy Spirit, it grasps spiritual things.

Continuing with his topic, Paul concludes the matter:

> *1 Corinthians 2:15-16*
> *"**15** But he that is spiritual judgeth all things, yet he himself is judged of no man. **16** For who hath known the mind of the Lord, that he may instruct him? But we have the mind of Christ."*

A believer, then, who is spiritual, judges or discerns all things. In other words, the spiritual discerns spiritual things. Paul, then, reminds believers that no one knows God's mind as to instruct God, or in other words, no person can advise God or give Him counsel, however, we can understand the things of God because God has given to believers, the mind of Messiah.

As a believer yields to that mind, they will understand spiritual things. Learning to yield to Messiah's mind might is wisdom. Of this topic, James, the apostle and first leader of the church at Jerusalem declared:

> *James 1:5-8*
> *"5 If any of you lack wisdom, let him ask of God, that giveth to all men liberally, and upbraideth not; and it shall be given him. 6 But let him ask in faith, nothing wavering. For he that wavereth is like a wave of the sea driven with the wind and tossed. 7 For let not that man think that he shall receive any thing of the Lord. 8 A double minded man is unstable in all his ways."*

In this passage, we can see that a person needs to recognize that they lack wisdom. After that recognition, there comes a request of God. God's response is not to scold, chastise or criticize the one in need of wisdom! God gives wisdom liberally to the seeker. However, James makes it clear, that the secret to receiving wisdom is to believe that God gives it. Otherwise, James says, their doubt is like a wave of the sea, driven and tossed. James concludes this is no way to receive from God. To be double-minded, produces instability.

Later, in the same book of James, the apostle tells believers how to recognize Godly wisdom:

Chapter 11
Chapter Analysis Basics

James 3:17-18
> "**17** But the wisdom that is from above is first pure, then peaceable, gentle, and easy to be intreated, full of mercy and good fruits, without partiality, and without hypocrisy. **18** And the fruit of righteousness is sown in peace of them that make peace."

Here are the earmarks of Godly wisdom:
- It is pure.
- It is peaceable.
- It is gentle.
- It is easy to be entreated, or willing to be discussed when it is shared.
- It is full of mercy.
- It is full of good fruits.
- It is without partiality, without prejudice.
- It is without hypocrisy, or a double standard.

Our first step, then in learning the skill of doing a Chapter Analysis, is to invite the Holy Spirit to help, and then to rely upon the God-given wisdom given as we dissect scripture passages and reassemble them, as well. As we do this procedure, we use what is called the ISRAEL Method. ISRAEL is an acronym for:

- Investigate
- Study
- Research

These three things fall into the category of OBSERVATIONS:

- Align
- Evaluate
- Live It Out

These three things fall into the category of CONCLUSIONS.

UNDER OBSERVATIONS:

INVESTIGATE

Read the scriptures to know its surface meaning. This picks up on the notes from the last chapter, under the heading, "READ IT CAREFULLY". There, we suggested when analysing a book of the Bible to read it repeatedly[55], and listen to it as often as possible, too. The point of course, is to grasp the entirety of the book, so that one can discover its overall content. Later, when dissecting the book, chapters and verses can be kept within their context.

---

[55] One might wonder how often they should read a book of the Bible. It depends upon the size of the book and how the Holy Spirit leads.

Chapter 11
Chapter Analysis Basics

STUDY

After reading and listening to the selected Bible book, when you are ready, begin your Chapter Analysis. To do this, find a way of importing the text of that Bible book into a format where you can print it. Then print it out. We'll call this step your PLATFORM. On your first read of your selected Bible book material in platform format, read it over to familiarize yourself with it and ensure in the transfer to platform format that every chapter and verse was included.

Next, take coloured markers or crayons in hand, and read each chapter, one at a time. As you read it, look for repeated items and circle them. Often, certain repeated words in the translation might not be related in the original language of the transcripts. Check with a concordance to see the original word. This is to ensure theories which come forth, hold true in the original language.

Additionally, look for other things such as:
- Indicators of God:
    - Look for the information about the Godhead:
        - The Father.
        - The Son.
        - The Holy Spirit.
- Indicators of Main Characters

- o This could be the author, or a prophet, a king, or any person involved in the story.
- Indicators of Tribes, or Territories or Nations.
  - o This could be mentions of a tribe such as Benjamin, or a nation such as Israel, or Edom, or others.
- Indicators of Time.
  - o It could be the mention of in the first year of a King, or in a time after an earthquake.
- Indicators of Certain Subjects.
  - o There may be portions which suggest certain behaviours, or speak of certain doctrines, or other subjects such as idolatry.
- Indicators of Moral or Immoral Behaviours.
- Indicators of Promises or Coming Judgments and their reasons for coming.
- Indicators of the Day of LORD.
- And any other indicators that the Spirit shows you. These vary widely throughout the Bible and hence are too many to list here.

Do this marking in every chapter throughout the entire Bible book.

RESEARCH

At this point, you are ready to explore passages of interest. You might find a word, a custom, or a riddle,

Chapter 11
Chapter Analysis Basics

which you would like to research to determine its meaning in its original culture, first, and then determine if it is the same, today. Adopting a Hebraic mindset is imperative, especially as you look at the feasts of YHVH! Your goal, with everything you explore it always to discover God's original intent.

There is no limit to the time it might take, or the number of items you research. Simply know that the stages of a chapter analysis are time consuming and the more effort you put into it, the more benefit you will reap from it. Next, you will recap all the information you researched to tabulate it.

UNDER CONCLUSIONS:

ALIGN
With everything dissected, the next job is to reassemble the evidence *without any form of distortion*. Here, a student watches grammar tenses. Ensure integrity of the text, ensuring context remains intact. Here, also, is the place where Historical[56], Cultural and Instructional Content comes into play. Remembering these things help to keep the context.

---

[56] Points given in Chapter 10.

EVALUATE

At this stage, it is time to ensure that everything you concluded relates to other principles in the Word of God, especially within the two major themes of the Bible.

About Alignment and Evaluation

In this stage, you recap all the information you collected. Recapping is another skill that comes with time and with repeated practice. Keep in mind; to recap all your findings, it is best to do so one chapter at a time. If a theme moves from one chapter to another, note it.

To recap your findings, prepare lists of repeated words, phrases, ideas, themes, people's actions, etc. In short, whatever you discovered, put into comprehensive lists on every subject that stood out to you. As you compile your lists, when assembled, they give clarity as to the big idea of the book, as well as other themes.

Remember: your newly discovered information must fit within the whole counsel of God, including within the two major themes of the Bible. That helps to keep things in context.

Chapter 11
Chapter Analysis Basics

Dear Reader, this is an acquired skill. It takes time. It is *beyond the basic level of Bible Study*. We present the matter, here, for two reasons:
1. To show you that there is a way that you can study the Bible in depth, *on your own*, using a chapter analysis.
2. To invite you to try and do the beginnings of it. Should you want to learn it, begin it and grow into it, one step at a time.

Just remember, it is a powerful tool, and like all tools, it comes with a learning curve. Each student's learning curve is different!

LIVE IT OUT
Here is where the rubber meets the road! Truths learned are meant to be embraced.

On the last page of this Chapter, we present this information in Chart form. Note: the bottom rows show how all our studies work. The Workbook gives opportunity to explore the scriptures, and then, the textbook reaffirms the findings.

HERMENEUTICS
Hermeneutics is a term to describe the knowledge used to understand certain topics. As this book presented the basic techniques and safeguards of Bible

Study, please know that we presented principles of hermeneutics, made easy.

So now, dear reader, when you go to study and employ what this book presented, you can know that you have some of the early and basic principles of hermeneutics under your belt.

Chapter 11
Chapter Analysis Basics

CHART # 5: Inductive Style of Learning

CP & AA'S INDUCTIVE STYLE OF LEARNING
"A deeply personal and intimate approach to discovering biblical truth."

STEP # 1: PRAY	Invite the Holy Spirit to be your teacher.
STEP # 2: RI/CALL	Remember to utilize hermeneutic principles of scripture investigation.
STEP # 3: USE ISRAEL METHOD	Investigate, Study, Research, Align, Evaluate, Live out (as shown below).

THE ISRAEL METHOD

	OBSERVATIONS (Gather the evidence.)			CONCLUSIONS (Tabulate the discoveries.)	
I	**S**	**R**	**A**	**E**	**L**
INVESTIGATE	STUDY	RESEARCH	ALIGN	EVALUATE	LIVE OUT
Read the scripture to know its surface meaning.	Reassess the passage to determine its primary message.	Explore the scriptures in their Hebraic/Greek & cultural context.	Reassemble the evidence into the context of the verse, chapter, and intentions of the book.	Evaluate how the discovery relates to other principles in the Word of God	Live out the truth learned by embracing, and applying it in your life
	LOOK FOR THE TRUTH			ALIGN WITH THE TRUTH	
DISCOVER THE CONTENT.	DISCOVER THE BIG IDEA.	DISCOVER GOD'S ORIGINAL INTENTIONS.	CATALOGUE THE INFORMATION WITHIN THE WHOLE COUNSEL OF GOD.		IMPLEMENT THE WORD INTO YOUR LIFE.
The Workbook guides students through the first three stages.			*The Textbook* reaffirms the findings in light of the topic at hand.		

COPYRIGHT CP & AA 2024

Don't forget, the workbook has an extra chapter which presents a hands-on teaching on doing a chapter analysis. Do it before or after doing the conclusion. It is your choice.

CONCLUSION

We began this book by discussing the unique characteristics of God's living Word, especially its ability to divide soul and spirit asunder. Additionally, we mentioned a method of Bible Study called Inductive, expressing to the reader its overall learning style intended to keep the joy of discovery in learning. Along with those properties, we brought forth two goals of inductive Bible Study, namely:

- To encourage a close relationship with the Holy Spirit, and
- To give opportunity for a learning style that propagates explorative learning.

Included was a chapter encouraging the reader to meet with the author of the Bible, God, whenever they study.

In the last chapter, we explained a Chapter Analysis, along with the acronym, Israel, and ended the chapter with a chart recapping inductive style learning.

Bible Study Basics
A Closer Look at God's Word

Sandwiched in between the beginning and the end of this book, we discussed major things to keep in mind when taking a closer look at God's Word:
- Major Theme of the Bible, God Is.
- Major Theme of the Bible, Redemption.

Within the discussion of the Second Major Theme, Redemption, we spoke about the importance of the 7th Day, which is this present age, and the coming age, and the Day of the Lord that separated them.

Next, we looked at the books in the Bible, first in their canonical order and then in their Hebraic order. We looked at learning Biblical precepts, precept upon precept, line upon line. We spoke of the need to possess a commitment to study God's Word, and for that determination to grow day after day as one reads the Word and draws near to God.

From there, we spoke of Bible Study wisdom and techniques, emphasizing one more time the purpose of doing a deeper study. We mentioned, with fair warning, that technical details can easily overwhelm the study. We stressed the importance not to forget the purpose of the study in the first place: *getting to know God and His ways.* We concluded that chapter with a reminder to make the Holy Spirit the teacher and admonished all to listen to Him.

A NOTE FROM THE AUTHOR OF THIS BOOK
Dear reader.

I have studied the Word of God for over 40 years, learning as the Holy Spirit taught me. Every Bible Study I did, as the study began, I learned for my private life. I never intended to share the information gleaned other than for a sermon or something similar. However, the Holy Spirit had other plans. He wanted the information available to others.

In writing this book, I'd like to tell you something personal. This book, more than any of the others books I have written, stretched me the most. Partly, because I wanted to put the hermeneutics principles in the book in a different fashion. You see, I learned those principles through the help of the Holy Spirit, and did not really know they were called hermeneutic principles. I struggled with presenting them without terminology and in some kind of order. However, the Holy Spirit instructed me to relate them to others as He taught them to me.

Also, this book, with its contents on how to study the Bible, stretched me since my Holy Spirit training for it spanned a lot of years. During that time, I never took notes, but just enjoyed the learning, obeying the promptings of the Holy Spirit. When the Holy Spirit led me to begin the book, I found the task over whelming. However, everyone can learn something from that struggle. If learning and doing these things in the book took some time, and it took some time to understand how to present it in understandable format, then doing what is in the book will take some time to learn, too.

So please, dear reader, don't try to master this art of studying the Bible, immediately and certainly not in one sitting. Give yourself some time to learn the skill, for after all, the Bible is a good sized book! Remember what Isaiah, the prophet said:

Isaiah 28:10
"For precept must be upon precept, precept upon precept; line upon line, line upon line; here a little, and there a little:"

Whether it is one verse, one chapter or one book, the principles in this book all work the same, so start with a small piece of scripture you can handle. Also, be sure to use the accompanying Workbook for this course to walk you through it. Make yourself lots of notes from this book and the Workbook, too. Be confident that YHVH wants you to learn. Remember, the Holy Spirit will help you as He helped me.

Many blessings

APPENDIX

A Name to Honour
יְהֹוָה
YeHoVaH[57]

If, today, someone asked you to tell them the name of your earthly father, without hesitation you would declare it. If, for some reason, you did not know the identity of your earthly father, you would say so. You might even give an explanation as to why that might be so. Thus said, if asked to relate the name of your heavenly Father, today, would you do so with ease, or would you draw a blank?

Most of Christendom, today, is ignorant *as to the name of the Father*, as well as the way to pronounce it. As the author of this book, I would like to join the ranks of those who wish to relate that name to the world. I believe that when we stand before the Father on the day that we give an account for our deeds in this body, it would be a good thing to know His Son, His Name!

---

[57] Based on information given by Michael Rood. Some from his work entitled, The Chronological Bible, and some from his YouTube videos. For more information see page 28 of the Chronological Bible.

About The Name

Did you know that the name of the Father appears at least 6,828 times in the Hebrew scriptures? Scribes recorded it with four specific Hebrew letters. They are as follows:

י	Pronounced yode, or yod
ה	Pronounced as hey
ו	Pronounced as vav
ה	Pronounced as hey

For centuries, whenever the Jews come across these 4 letters they simply say, Adonai, or Ha Shem (meaning the name). They refuse to pronounce the name for several reasons, some of which we will look at momentarily. For now, let us look at whether their tradition affected Christianity. That we can easily do by looking at our Bibles to see the 4-letter name of the Father either written or substituted.

A quick look reveals that our KJV Bibles, as well as many other versions, the 4-letter name presented to readers is a 4-letter English word, "YeHoVaH". [58] [59] Whether intentional or not, Christendom has followed the ancient tradition of the Jews.

---

[58] In some translations it is GOD.
[59] We also can shorten that name to YHVH (Yod, Heh, Vav, Heh)

An Ancient Tradition

In early second century times[60] Rabbis hid the pronunciation of the holy name of God. They did this by omitting the vowel pointings, which are necessary to make the name pronounceable. Hence, as they carefully wrote the scriptures, their omittance of the vowel pointings made the name unpronounceable. Historians believe there were two reasons why they did this:

i. According to Josephus, Rome, under the rule of Domitian, 81 to 96 CE, put to death anyone using the name of the Jewish or Christian God.

ii. Many believe that the Rabbis borrowed a tradition from pagans, whereby the name of their god was considered too holy to mention, so they called him "Ba-al" meaning Lord. The Jews adopted this practice and most still practice it today, even some Messianic Jews!

Tradition Continues

Bible translators followed their tradition for many reasons which are not presently known. It is possible, they forgot the pronunciation of the name, but more than likely, those who knew it, hid it.[61]. Whatever the reason, following this tradition caused Christians to continue in this tradition.

---

[60] Some scholars even dating further back.
[61] According to some, the Jews secretly knew the name.

Does that tradition offend the Heavenly Father?
If indeed its origin was Baal worship, then we can give a resounding Amen to the fact it offends God. In addition, as we look at scripture, we see the Apostle, Peter, declaring that "whosoever shall call upon the name of YHVH[62] shall be saved.[63]" Clearly God desires that all, including the Gentiles, come to Him[64] for salvation.

An Historic Discovery
Today, some Hebrew scholars[65] have searched the world over for Hebrew manuscripts. In doing so, they found many Hebrew documents have the full name with vowels and therefore the pronunciation of the name. These scholars may different slightly in pronunciation, but nevertheless, they are making the name of YeHoVaH known today.

Our Saviour's Name Hidden in This Name
In looking at the Hebrew root of the name of the Father, pronounced *Yah-Ho **Vah'***, and looking at another scripture, we see something amazing about

---

[62] In a moment you will see that YHVH's Name is in our Saviour's Name.

[63] *Joel 2:32; Acts 2:21*

[64] If they call upon the name of YJVH, surely the Father will show them Yeshua! *Romans 10:12-15*

[65] Nehemiah Gordon, a Hebrew scholar, according to his testimony on his website continues to mention increasing numbers of incidents in manuscripts where the name of God with all vowel appointments appears.

our Saviour. In speaking of the Prophet, the one the Father would send and to whom all must listen and obey, YeHoVaH said that His name would be in the name of the Prophet.

Exodus 23:21 "Beware of him, and obey his voice, provoke him not; for he will not pardon your transgressions[66]: for my name [is] in him".

Our Saviour's name, as given by the angel was "Yehoshua", which means Salvation.

That name, with its Hebrew letters reads as:

י	Pronounced yode or yod
ה	Pronounced hey
ו	Pronounced vav
ש	Pronounced shin
ע	Pronounced ayin

The name of the Father (יְהֹוָה) is in the name of the Son! The first three letters of YeHoVaH show it! (Yod, Heh, Vav). Is it so amazing that the name of our Father is in the true name of the One YeHoVaH sent to redeem us!

Honour the Father's Name

Throughout this book, and all later books, as well as all accompanying audios and PowerPoints, it is the

---

[66] Please keep in mind that Yeshua bore the punishment for your sins. Your sins were not pardoned in the sense no punishment was paid. Yeshua atoned for them on your behalf!

author's intention to widely use, proclaim and continually pronounce the name of the Father, as well as the name of Yeshua. Indeed, this breaks with tradition of many, however, thus far as we have shared the news of the Father's name and use Yeshua's birth name, reception has been excellent.

Name Challenge

Since, as of this reading, you are no longer ignorant of your heavenly Father's name, we invite you to join the unofficial network of proclaimers of the Father's name and shout it from the house tops. In doing so, you honour the Heavenly Father, our Savour Yeshua, and the Holy Spirit.

> *Romans 10:12-15*
> *"12 For there is no difference between the Jew and the Greek: for the same Lord over all is rich unto all that call upon him. 13 For whosoever shall call upon the name of YeHoVaH shall be saved. 14 How then shall they call on him in whom they have not believed? and how shall they believe in him of whom they have not heard? and how shall they hear without a preacher? 15 And how shall they preach, except they be sent? as it is written, How beautiful are the feet of them that preach the gospel of peace and bring glad tidings of good things!"*

ABOUT THE KING JAMES VERSION

Scriptures quoted in this book *originate* from the KJV **public domain version** of the Bible, which means, no copyright exists on this version of the scripture. While some find this translation outdated, Jeanne, trained in the KJV still finds this version helpful, and uses it in all her books[67].

In using KJV, however, it is good to remember the following:
- Some words in the KJV have changed meaning over the centuries. To understand such words, look up the root word in its original language. In doing so, the meaning stands out. For example. KJV uses the word "conversation" however, in its original language it means moral character, or behaviour.
- When KJV spoke of humanity, they said, "humankind". When you read that word, or hear others speak about the scriptures using the term, "humankind", know it refers to all humankind, not a specific gender.

Due to tradition, the name of the Father, YeHoVaH appears as LORD, or at times as Jehovah. However, in all Jeanne's manuscripts, YeHoVaH or YHVH replaces the term LORD.

---

[67] In later manuscripts, the author updated the more archaic words in the KJV such as wouldest or couldest.

SALVATION'S MESSAGE

Yeshua, when walking on earth, said this:
John 3:14-18
> 14 And as Moses lifted up the serpent in the wilderness, even so must the Son of man be lifted up: 15 That whosoever believes in him should not perish but have eternal life. 16 For God so loved the world, that he gave his only begotten Son, that whosoever believes in him should not perish, but have everlasting life. 17 For God sent not his Son into the world to condemn the world; but that the world through him might be saved. 18 He that believes on him is not condemned: but he that believes not is condemned already, because he hath not believed in the name of the only begotten Son of God.

During the time of Moses, the children of Israel in the wilderness, rebelled against God, at which time poisonous serpents infiltrated the camp, killing many of the people. After seeking YeHoVaH for a solution to the problem, Moses followed God's instructions and made a bronze serpent fashioned and erected it on a pole in sight of the people. Whosoever wanted to live, must acknowledge their rebellion against YeHoVaH, and in doing so, look upon the erected pole and bronze serpent, to YeHoVaH, who gave them life in place of death, then they would live.

Yeshua said, just as Moses erected that bronze serpent in the wilderness, He would be lifted for all to see. This referred to the event, in the future, of Yeshua's crucifixion. During the time when the serpent hung on that pole, whosoever wanted to live and not die from the serpent's bite must acknowledge their rebellion, their sin against YeHoVaH.

Likewise, for those who wish to live eternally, they must look upon the cross of the crucified One, to Yeshua, who provided life for them. This was an act of love for all humankind, necessary because man is born from Adam, and thus is born with an inherent sin.

Secondly, man sins. The consequence of sin is death, and eternal death, wherein man will spend an eternity in darkness, away from YeHoVaH. Unfortunately, there is nothing humanly possible to reverse those consequences. Even if a person had made a genuine decision never to sin again, and for some reason they succeeded, all their good deeds and good living would not erase the penalty of eternal death.

There is only *one way* for Eternal Life to touch a person's life. That way, Yeshua explained to His listeners, comes *through the cross.*

Salvation comes by understanding these facts:
1. Yeshua, being the Son of God and the fulfilment of the scriptures, never sinned.

2. YeHoVaH, on behalf of every human being on the earth, chose to make Yeshua become as sin, in His Eyes, so that Yeshua might pay the penalty for sin, for all of humanity.
3. Yeshua paid that penalty. He died on the cross and was buried in a tomb.
4. Three days later, He rose again, appearing to His disciples, to show them the reality of His resurrection, to show them God vindicated Him and made Him both Lord and Messiah.
5. Yeshua could not stay in the tomb, because "death" comes to all who sin, but since Yeshua never sinned, therefore, death could not hold Him in the grave.
6. All those who come to Yeshua, to receive Him as their Saviour, receive liberty from sin and from its horrible consequence, eternal death.
7. They enter YeHoVaH's Kingdom and receive eternal life, as well as another gift: The Righteousness of Messiah. After salvation, when YeHoVaH looks upon a believer in Messiah, He sees Yeshua's perfect life and sees a redeemed believer, set aside for YeHoVaH. Since salvation has taken place in the believer, the Holy Spirit dwells within them.
8. All it takes to receive salvation from YeHoVaH is receiving His Messiah, fully repenting from

sinning against God[68]. YeHoVaH even gives the believer the faith to receive His gift of Salvation!

The Apostle Paul put it this way:

Ephesians 2:8
"For by grace are ye saved through faith; and that not of yourselves: it is the gift of God"

When you pray the following prayer, realize we present it here to get you started in your walk with YeHoVaH. Living out your salvation depends upon your commitment to follow through *from this point, onward*. From the moment of your commitment and onward, dear one, please seek YeHoVaH for His help in all things, including help to make your life align with truth, and in the end be a praise unto His name, forever!

SINNER'S PRAYER
& LIFETIME COMMITMENT

Heavenly, Father:

I acknowledge before You, YeHoVaH, that I am a sinner. I understand sin's punishment is a life without You, for all eternity. Thank You for sending Yeshua to the earth, as the Messiah. I understand now that He died in my place, to take my punishment for my sins. I believe You raised Yeshua from the dead, and now

---

[68] *And against man. When a person steals, etc. they sin against both God and man. PLEASE NOTE: all references to "man", either by scripture or the author, refers to all humankind, not a specific gender.*

that I accepted Him as my personal Saviour, my old life dies, and my new life begins.

I humbly ask You to forgive me of my sins, and as of this moment, I receive Yeshua as my Saviour. I open my heart to receive the works of the cross that You provided for me through Yeshua, and with Your help, I will walk away from my sin, turning my back upon my own will and ways. I will now live my life seeking to obey Your Word and Your will. Help me to live, from this point onward, in a manner pleasing to You.

One more thing:
Remember, this gospel message comes with power. When you hear it, the Kingdom of God draws near to you. When you repent of your sins and receive Salvation, the Kingdom of God moves within. You cannot see it, feel it, or tell it from an outward observance. It is accepted, received, and lived out by faith! Seek out other believers in Messiah and may God bless you richly as you live your life, now, completely for Him!

So now, be sure and tell someone!
Remember that a person believes with the heart unto righteousness and confesses with their mouth unto salvation, as spoken about in *Romans 10:10*":
> *"10 For with the heart man believes unto righteousness; and with the mouth confession is made unto salvation*

SCRIPTURE INDEX

1

1 Corinthians 2:12-14 151
1 Corinthians 2:15-16 153
1 John 2:26-29 143
1 Peter 2:12 59
1 Thessalonians 4:11-12
.... 134

2

2 Chronicles 20:7 125
2 Peter 3:9 .... 90, 95
2 Timothy 2:15 .... 4, 134
2 Timothy 3:16 ..... 91, 137
2 Timothy 4:1-4 135

A

Acts 2:16-21 87
Acts 2:21 174

C

Colossians 2:16-17 51
Colossians 3:15-16 142

D

Daniel 11:32 b 193
Daniel 3:1-30 92
Daniel 5:23-24 53
Daniel 5:26-28 54
Daniel 6: 7-24 92
Deuteronomy 28:13 106
Deuteronomy 30:14 139
Deuteronomy 31:25-26 .25
Deuteronomy 4:29 133
Deuteronomy 5:6-7 21

E

Ecclesiastes 12:11-13 9
Ecclesiastes 12:9-12 130
Ephesians 2:6 28
Ephesians 2:8 181
Ephesians 2:8-9 29
Exodus 23:21...............175
Exodus 24: 6-8 26

G

Galatians 3:24 25
Genesis 1:1 a 36
Genesis 1:13 66
Genesis 1:1-3 37
Genesis 1:19 66
Genesis 1:2....................42
Genesis 1:23 66
Genesis 1:26-27.............40
Genesis 1:3 38
Genesis 1:31 ....66, 70

Genesis 1:5 66
Genesis 1:8 66
Genesis 2:1-3 67
Genesis 2:2-3 45
Genesis 3:12-13 42
Genesis 3:14 69
Genesis 3:15 43
Genesis 3:17 69
Genesis 3:21 49
Genesis 3:8 42

H

Habakkuk 2:20 137
Hebrews 10: 4-10 26
Hebrews 11:6 130
Hebrews 12:22-24 23
Hebrews 12:23 28
Hebrews 12:24 27
Hebrews 4:12 .. 11, 16, 129
Hebrews 8:5 51
Hebrews 8:7 99
Hebrews 9:27 55
Hosea 10:12 134

I

Isaiah 10:1-3 56
Isaiah 10:3 58
Isaiah 13:10-13 80
Isaiah 13:6-9 79
Isaiah 2:12-18 78

Isaiah 28:10 168
Isaiah 28:10 a) 115
Isaiah 28:9-13 116
Isaiah 29:13 ....117, 123
Isaiah 34:1-4 82
Isaiah 41:4 36
Isaiah 44:6 45
Isaiah 48:12-13 39
Isaiah 48:17-19 140
Isaiah 54:11-14 140
Isaiah 55:11 12
Isaiah 55:6 133

J

James 1:5-8 154
James 2:23 126
James 3:17-18 155
Jeremiah 31:31 .....107, 112
Jeremiah 31:31-34 110
Joel 1: 15-20 83
Joel 2:10-11 85
Joel 2:1-9 84
Joel 2:25 77
Joel 2:27-31 86
Joel 2:32 174
John 13:35 113
John 14:25-27 142
John 16:8 14
John 3:14-18 178
John 5:17 ....46, 67

John 5:39 95
John 6:63 .... 11, 138
Joshua 22:5 119
Joshua 23:11 30

M

Malachi 3:6 45
Mark 12:30-31 54
Mark 7:18-23 122
Mark 7:21-23 13
Matthew 12:32 .... 71, 77
Matthew 13:45-46 118
Matthew 22:37-40 ..... 112, 113
Matthew 24:29-31 89
Matthew 27:50-53 88

P

Proverbs 16:18 29
Proverbs 4:20-22 .. 10, 106
Proverbs 4:23 123
Proverbs 6:23 106
Psalm 1:1-3 107
Psalm 104:5 35
Psalm 105:1 30
Psalm 119:111 31
Psalm 119:12-16 124
Psalm 119:129 31
Psalm 119:140-144 53

Psalm 119:1-5 120
Psalm 119:16 99
Psalm 119:168 31
Psalm 119:18 130
Psalm 119:24 31
Psalm 119:30 129
Psalm 119:6-11 121
Psalm 136:1-8 96
Psalm 147:5 96
Psalm 19:14 47
Psalm 53:2 133
Psalm 66:18 30
Psalm 73:28 30
Psalm 81:3 108
Psalm 9: 7-10 75
Psalm 9:11-18 73
Psalm 90:2 37
Psalm 93:5 31

R

Revelation 13:8 ....48, 68
Revelation 21:1-5 71
Romans 10:10: 182
Romans 10:12-15 174, 176
Romans 11:23-29 189
Romans 3:23-26 22
Romans 5:12 44
Romans 5:18 68
Romans 8:18-22 49

CP & AA FAITH STATEMENT

ABOUT GOD:
We believe:
- *there is only One, True God.*
- *He is the God of Abraham, Isaac and Jacob.*
- *He is Omnipotent, Omniscient and Omnipresent.*
- *He is Eternal, Holy, Righteous and Immutable.*
- *the One True God is revealed to us as the "Godhead".*
- *in the manifestation as the Heavenly Father, as seen in the scriptures.*
- *in the manifestation of Incarnate Son of God, (Yeshua), as seen in the scriptures,*
- *in His virgin birth, in His sinless life, in His miracles, in His complete atoning sacrifice, in His bodily resurrection from the dead, in His ascension into heaven, and in His exalted position in heavenly places, whose Name is above all names.*
- *and in His future return (Second Coming) to the earth in power and in glory,*
- *in the Atoning Blood of the Living Son of God, Yeshua, is the only means by which a person can*

receive complete forgiveness and cleansing from sin.
- in the manifestation of the Holy Spirit, as seen in the scriptures.
- He is, therefore, not just an influence.
- He reproves the world of sin, of righteousness and of judgment to come.

ABOUT THE BIBLE:
We believe:
- the Bible is the inspired Word of God and in its original transcripts is infallible and authoritative.
- in the Equal Authority of both the Hebraic and Apostolic Scriptures (Old and New Covenant), understanding that the First (Old) Covenant concealed Yeshua, and the Second (New) Covenant revealed Him.

ABOUT BELIEVERS:
We believe:
- in the need for individual, personal repentance and in receiving, by faith, the work of the cross, believing with the heart unto righteousness and confessing with the mouth unto salvation.
- in the indwelling of the true believer by the Holy Spirit, guiding believers, and enabling them to develop the fruit of the Spirit, bringing them into a

place where they live a holy life to which all believers are called.
- *in the Baptism of the Holy Spirit whereby believers are empowered by God to live a holy life, given an ability to speak in an unknown language commonly called, "tongues", and are enabled to operate in the gifts of the Spirit.*
- *in Divine Healing as an integral part of the gospel message and the life of a believer.*

ABOUT THE FIRST & SECOND COVENANT:
We believe:
- *that the inauguration of the Second Covenant did not do away with, alter, remove or nullify that which God revealed through the First Covenant, which include God's Laws, precepts and commandments.*
- *that the Holy Spirit leads believers to know, understand and to obey God's Laws, precepts and commandments.*

ABOUT A FINAL JUDGMENT:
We believe:
- *in the resurrection and judgment of the saved and the lost.*
- *the saved go to everlasting life and the lost into everlasting damnation.*

ABOUT THE RAPTURE:
We believe:
- *in the Blessed Hope (Parousia or Rapture) of the earthly Body of Messiah (believers) at the last trumpet call.*

ABOUT ISRAEL:
We Believe:
- *all believers in Yeshua are grafted into the root of David (Israel) and thus is borne by the root and therefore positioned and entitled to the promises of God, neither nullifying Israel's importance, nor replacing Israel.*
- *in the Full Redemptive Power of God towards His People, Israel, and that, if they no longer remain in unbelief regarding Yeshua as Messiah, they shall be grafted in as specified in Romans 11:23-29.*

ABOUT OUR HEBRAIC HERITAGE:
We believe:
- *that we have a rich Hebraic Heritage, including, the Biblical Feasts of the Lord which are fulfilled by Yeshua, some at His First coming and some at His second,*
- *that believers in Messiah (Christ) are free to celebrate the feasts of YHVH in the same manner as the early, first century church celebrated them.*

BOOKS BY JEANNE METCALF

An Arsenal of Powerful Prayers [69]
  Scriptural Prayers to Move Mountains
Arising Incense
  A Believer's Priesthood
Above Artificial Intelligence
  Finding God in a World of A.I.
Bible Study Basics
  A Closer Look at God's Word
Candidate for A Miracle
  Wisdom from the Miracles of Yeshua
Foundations of Revival
  Biblical Evidence for Revival
His Reflection
  What God longs to see in His People
Heaven's Greater Government
  Behind the Scenes of Earth's Events
In The Name of Yehovah We Set Up Our Banners
  Biblical use of Banners
It's All About Heaven
  As Pictured in Scripture
Kingdom Keys for Kingdom Kids
  Walking in Kingdom Power
Molded for the Miraculous
  Why God made You

---

[69] This is a book of written prayers of assorted topics to help believers live a stronger, active faith. No workbook.

Our Secure Faith Heritage
Foundational Truths to an Unshakeable Walk with God

Releasing the Impossible
The Limitless Power of Intercession
Volume 1: Intercessions from the Author's Life
Volume 2: Intercessions from Biblical Characters
Workbook: Both Volumes compiled in Workbook.

Salvation Depicted in a Meal [70]
An Hebraic Christian Guide to Passover

The Jeremiah Generation
God's Response to Injustice

The Warrior Bride-
God's Kingdom Advancing through Spiritual Warfare

Thy Kingdom Come
Entering God's Rest in Prayer

Watching, Waiting, Warning
Obeying Yeshua's Command to Watch & Pray

When Nations Rumble
A Study of the Book of Amos

Worship in Spirit and In Truth [71]
The Tabernacle of David - Past, Present & Future

---

[70] Haggadah (Guide) for a Christian Passover. No Workbook.
[71] Good sister book to "In the Name of YeHoVaH We Set Up Our Banners".

ABOUT JEANNE METCALF

Jeanne believes the Word of God opens a door to help every believer to know their God. That knowledge, once gleaned and retained, makes strong believers to help them stand in the real world in which we live, no matter their vocation.

With these convictions in mind, Jeanne, inspired and led by the Holy Spirit, began to write in the 1990's. Soon she developed inductive[72] style Bible Studies and self-published them for her students to use. With her major goal to equip the saints, she found that her sound teachings, presented with clarity and simplicity, made an impact. As long as her listeners put in their valuable time to study scripture and took Jeanne's advice to call upon the Holy Spirit to help them, they became powerful believers, transformed, prepared and ready to stand in their generation.

---

[72] In the inductive Bible Study method, believers learn first by reading and studying the Word on their own, then they glean from the textbook. This study method often gives a better foundation to a believer's faith than sitting through lectures or speaker related teachings.

Today, past students who studied the Bible with Jeanne, as well current new students, testify as to the validity of Jeanne's writing and teaching gift. They love the clarity and simplicity of the Word as she presents it in a refreshing straightforward format. Thus, they encouraged Jeanne to make her books more widely available.

Therefore, Jeanne began Cegullah Publishing, and then a year later, opened Cegullah Apologetic Academy. The academy, in addition to presenting accredited, Bible Study material, invites all believers to read or study the Word of God, and thereby, be strong in YeHoVaH and the strength of His might.

A greater availability of Jeanne's works (as well as other authors which Cegullah Publishing looks forward to publishing in the future), opens doors for more people to know their God and do exploits!

"But the people that know their God shall be strong and do exploits". Daniel 11:32 b

***

i-Stock Pictures used in this book.	
Cover	1477629037
Man with Magnifying Glass	2104164120

APOLOGETICS ACADEMY
(CP & AA)

At CP & AA, we focus on God's Word.

We present that Word in three ways:
- for casual reading
- for unaccredited Bible Study
- for accredited Bible Study (degrees such as Bachelor, Master, Doctorate)

Our Vision is to supply Christian, Bible-based materials to help our readers to know, understand and grow in God's Word

Our Focus is to help our readers to know *what they believe and why.*

Our Mission is to provide biblically solid, educational tools to help our readers to know their God and connect with Him.

Our Publishing Motto:
Publishing the treasures of modern-day scribes.

Our Academy Motto:
Earnestly contend for the faith once given to the saints.

Your Invitation:

We invite you, dear reader, to the wonderful world of the Word of God.

Love it.   **Casually Read the Word**
Consider picking up any one of our Bible Studies. Enjoy the insights of the Word of God.

Learn it.   **Consider Inductive Learning**
Dig deep into the Word of God with our study tools, and with the help of the Holy Spirit. Discover truth for yourself.

(While you can do this unaccredited, we invite you to consider doing it for accreditation towards a degree.)

Live it out!   **Conform Your Life to The Truth**
After you uncover such great truths within God's Word, put what you learned into practice. In that way you become a doer of the Word!

CONTACT INFORMATION
www.cegullahpublishing.ca

www.ingramcontent.com/pod-product-compliance
Lightning Source LLC
Chambersburg PA
CBHW071202160426
43196CB00011B/2165